THE SHADOW ~~~~~~

Letters in Flames

Moshe Pelli

University Press of America,® Inc.
Lanham · Boulder · New York · Toronto · Plymouth, UK

Copyright © 2008 by
University Press of America,® Inc.
4501 Forbes Boulevard
Suite 200
Lanham, Maryland 20706
UPA Acquisitions Department (301) 459-3366

Estover Road
Plymouth PL6 7PY
United Kingdom

All rights reserved
Printed in the United States of America
British Library Cataloging in Publication Information Available

Library of Congress Control Number: 2007936086
ISBN-13: 978-0-7618-3915-6 (paperback : alk. paper)
ISBN-10: 0-7618-3915-1 (paperback : alk. paper)

Front cover photo: "Dark Light" by Shmuel Bak.
Back cover photo: "Smoke" by Mordechai Goldfarb.

♾™The paper used in this publication meets the minimum
requirements of American National Standard for Information
Sciences—Permanence of Paper for Printed Library Materials,
ANSI Z39.48—1984

For my granddaughter, Ariel

Contents

גוילין נשרפים ואתיות פורחות
The parchments burned but the letters soar upward
Talmud Bavli, Avodah Zarah, 18a

Preface

‏"גוילין נשרפים ואותיות פורחות"‏
"The parchments burned but the letters soar upward"
Talmud Bavli, Avodah Zarah, 18a

In the classical story of the ten Jewish martyrs, the Talmud tells of Rabbi Hanina ben Tradion (100–135 CE), who was caught by the Romans teaching the Torah in defiance of Emperor Hadrian's decrees; they wrapped him in the parchments of the Torah scroll, placed firewood on him and set him on fire. His disciples asked him, "Rabbi, what do you see?" and he replied, "Parchments that are burning but the letters soar upward."

This paradigmatic story of Jewish history and Hanina's proverbial phrase was floating before me as I was working on this book, *The Shadow of Death: Letters in Flame*"; its title alluding to it and to the *Psalms* 23 verse.

•

Emerging from the shadow of death, survivors of the Hurban (Destruction), as it was called then, left Europe for safer shores in the newly established State of Israel, the U.S., and some other countries. Those who came to Israel searched for their families – for their only relatives who were alive because they lived in pre-state Israel during the war. Some of our surviving relatives stayed with my family for several months until they moved on and rebuilt their lives in the new Jewish state. Some even fought their second war for survival.

This was my first encounter with the aftermath of the Holocaust.

•

They told their stories of survival and the story of those who did not survive. Their stories were personal testimonies, partially told, mostly untold. Memories were hurtful – to use a phrase from one of Aharon Appelfeld's short

9

stories – and many of the survivors were mostly silent. It was silence that spoke the loudest for them.

As youngsters in the 1940s, we did not hear this silence. Neither did we listen attentively when these survivors did tell their stories. For some time, a similar silence was also the dominant tone in the main corpus of Hebrew literature, and consequently, in Hebrew literary criticism.

•

The realization of what survivors in my family endured came only later. To me, it came when I visited Poland in 1998 and went to the site of Sobibor concentration camp. What remained of the camp is a modest museum which commemorates the story of the successful uprising against the Nazis. Immediately after the uprising the Nazis destroyed the camp altogether.

In the museum's display of nineteen pictures of inmates who led the uprising, I suddenly saw a familiar face, and under the picture there was the name Goldfarb; not even a first name. He was my cousin, who came to live with us in Israel in 1948. I provided them his first name: Mordechai....

Some of his stories that remained in vague memory surfaced then and there, real and vivid, as if made of sights and not of words.

He was an artist and was kept alive because of his talent in painting signs. In the later part of his life in Israel he devoted his time to painting. See his biography in the end of the book and his art on the back cover.

•

More awareness of the impact of the Holocaust on my immediate family came on that visit to Poland as I was searching for my family roots and went to see my parents' hometown of Piaski Lubelski, near Lublin.

It was a journey back in time. I returned to visit a place where I had not been before except in faded stories and reconstructed memories – not my own, but of resurrected lives, based on the family album. Both my parents' families – grandparents, uncles and aunts, cousins, nieces and nephews – perished in the Holocaust. We grew up as a single-generation family, cut off from its tree roots.

What remained of the family are parched pictures and letters soaring upward.

And then I went to Auschwitz and Maidanek, sites of the Holocaust, and saw what had happened to the other trees in the forest that were consumed in the fire.

•

Twenty-five years after the silence, the memories emerged in the form of memoirs, testimonials, resurrected stories, poems, and various other types of Holocaust writings. Today there is a substantial body of writing by survivors, second-generation survivors, and others, which are referred to as literature of the Holocaust – the subject of my book.

The book is divided into two main sections of Holocaust writings. The first is 'The Holocaust Experience From Within' – analyses of literary works by survivors who experienced the Holocaust first-hand. Among them, Aharon Appelfeld, Elie Wiesel, Primo Levi, Ka-tzetnik, and Jerzy Kosinski. Their works were written in several languages: Hebrew, Yiddish, French, Italian, and English. The second section is devoted to 'After the Holocaust – Experience from Without,' namely, literary analysis of works by writers who responded to the Holocaust after the event. They are the Israeli writers Hanoch Bartov, Hayim Gouri, and Yehuda Amichai who wrote in Hebrew (see brief biographies in the back of the book). All their works have been translated into English. The book is literary oriented, thus the focus and emphasis on textual and literary analysis of major examples of literature of the Holocaust.

•

I have been writing this book for many years, ever since I began to teach a course on the literature of the Holocaust in Hebrew and Jewish literature at several universities. I have published articles and presented papers and lectures on this subject throughout the years, notably a series of lectures at Melbourne University in Australia in the summers of 1978 and 1979. Interestingly, a final reading of the manuscript was done in June 2007 during another visit to Melbourne....

The book presents some aspects of these authors and their writings. It does not purport to be a comprehensive study of either Holocaust literature – although it deals with the concept and its literary aspects – or the authors.

It is an act of memory – of a memorial – of my immediate family who perished as well as the larger family of Jewish people and others who were victims of Nazism.

Even though the parchments were consumed in the conflagration in Europe, their letters – those that emerged in survivors' writings, testimonies, and memoirs, and non-survivors' literary renditions – continue to soar upward for humanity to remember and to learn the message.

•

Upon completing the book, I would like to express my gratitude to Shmuel Bak, noted artist, for allowing me to use his very impressive work "Dark Light" for the cover of the book. I would also like to thank the Holocaust Memorial Resource and Education Center of Central Florida, and its founder and president, Tess Wise, and her husband, Abe, for their support and enlightened discussions on the Holocaust, Judaism, and Israel. Also, I would like to acknowledge my gratitude to many students who were the first readers of this book before it was even written. I extend my thanks to Nathaniel James Rhodes, Leeat Shnaider, Brooke Goldberg, and Anat Taggart for assisting in the preparation of the manuscript, and to Merrille R. Koffler and Dr. Kurt Koerting for their helpful comments.

Moshe Pelli
University of Central Florida, Orlando, Fl.
June-July 2007

Introduction
"Poetry after Auschwitz"?

Upon approaching the subject of literary portrayal of the Holocaust, one feels that words are too weak a medium to convey and relate the experience and the meaning of the Holocaust in an authentic way. For a moment, one would like to substitute silence for the most expressive words. For how can human language even attempt to convey the suffering, the atrocities, the cruelty – the total inhumanity and bestiality – that epitomized the Holocaust?

Indeed, the question is raised as to whether the Holocaust experience lends itself to any form of artistic expression. It was the critic T. W. Adorno who expressed this notion in his proverbial phrase, "to write poetry after Auschwitz is barbaric."[1] Commenting on Adorno's phrase, the critic and student of the literature of atrocity, Lawrence L. Langer, posed the question in his book *The Holocaust and the Literary Imagination*, "How should art – how can art? – represent the inexpressibly inhuman suffering of the victims, without doing an injustice to that art?"[2] Langer further stated that "There is something disagreeable, almost dishonorable, in the conversion of the suffering of the victims into works of art" (p. l).

George Steiner, another student of the Holocaust and of language and literature, asserted in his book *Language and Silence* "that the reality of the Holocaust addresses the contemporary mind most effectively with the

---

1. Theodor W. Adorno, *Noten zur Literatur, Gesammelte Schriften*, II (Frankfurt A/M, 1974), S. 422: "...nach Auschwitz noch Lyrik zu schreiben, sei barbarisch." Adorno's book has been translated into English. See *Notes to Literature*, II (New York, 1992), pp. 87–88, chapter on "Commitment."
2. Lawrence L. Langer, *The Holocaust and the Literary Imagination* (New Haven, 1975), p. 1. Pages cited in parentheses in the text in this chapter and other chapters refer to a source discussed in that context and referred to in a related footnote.

authority of silence." It is his view that "The world of Auschwitz lies outside speech as it lies outside reason."[3]

Rejecting this plea for silence, the German poet and critic Hans Magnus Enzensberger argued that "surrender to silence would be surrender to cynicism, and would thus by implication [be] a concession to the very forces that had created Auschwitz in the first place."[4]

Alvin H. Rosenfeld, a critic and student of Holocaust literature, also argued against silence. He quoted Elie Wiesel's statement rejecting the concept of 'literature of the Holocaust,' saying that

There is no such thing as a literature of the Holocaust, nor can there be. The very expression is a contradiction in terms. Auschwitz negates any form of literature, as it defies all systems, all doctrines.... A novel about Auschwitz is not a novel, or else it is not about Auschwitz. The very attempt to write such a novel is blasphemy.

Rosenfeld pointed out that Elie Wiesel himself did not embrace silence in his own writings about the Holocaust, and that "to let silence prevail would be tantamount to granting Hitler one more posthumous victory."[5]

On this point of artistic representation of the Holocaust, Langer contended that "the validity of Adorno's apprehension that art's transfiguration of moral chaos into aesthetic form might in the end misrepresent that chaos and create a sense of meaning and purpose in the experience of the Holocaust (and hence, paradoxically, a justification of it in aesthetic terms) depends very much on how the artist exploits his material [...] and on the methods he employs to involve the sensibilities of his audience in the world of his imagination" (p. 2).

Langer asserted that what is involved in works of art on the Holocaust "is not the transfiguration of empirical reality [...] but its *dis*figuration." That is to say, "the conscious and deliberate alienation of the reader's sensibilities from the world of the usual and familiar, with an accompanying infiltration into the work of the grotesque, the senseless, and the unimaginable, to such a degree that the possibility of aesthetic pleasure as Adorno conceives of it is intrinsically eliminated" (pp. 2–3).

Langer continues, thus "the will of the reader is drawn into the autonomous milieu of the work of art and is subtly transformed – disfigured [...] – until it is compelled to recognize, to 'see' imaginatively both the relationship between the empirical reality of the Holocaust and its artistic

---

3. George Steiner, *Language and Silence* (New York, 1967), p. 127.
4. Adorno cites Enzensberger in his book mentioned in note 1, S. 423; the English version, pp. 87–88. The translation here is Langer's, *The Holocaust and the Literary Imagination*, p. 2.
5. Alvin H. Rosenfeld, *A Double Dying: Reflections on Holocaust Literature* (Bloomington, 1980), p. 14. He quotes from Wiesel's article in *Sh'ma* magazine published in 1975.

representation in the work of literature, *and* the fundamental distinction between both of these worlds and the nonvictim orientation of this will" (of the reader). Thus, "the reader is temporarily an insider and permanently an outsider, and the very tension resulting from this paradox precludes the possibility of the kind of 'pleasure' Adorno mentions" (p. 3).

Langer argued that "the uncertain nature of the experience recorded, combined with the reader's feeling of puzzled involvement in it, prohibits Adorno's fear that the reader may discern in the inconceivable fate of the victims 'some sense after all.' As we shall see, the principle of aesthetic stylization itself prohibits it" (p. 3).

This is a summary of Langer's views about the kind of literature that may attempt to come close to depicting the Holocaust. His seminal observations were published in 1975. They indicate the complexities involved in the treatment of the Holocaust in works of literary art.

It seems that most sensitive people would not accept silence as the answer to the literary expression of the Holocaust. Limitation of language to express the full meaning of the Holocaust notwithstanding, resorting to utter silence would be tantamount to humanity's psychological suppression of this traumatic event. It will further indicate a desire to disregard the Holocaust, and may point to an inability to fathom its significance and implication. Silence may undermine the need to reach some somber conclusions about the potential for evil of the human race.

Why not, then, confine discussion on the Holocaust just to the domain of history, to the "mere factual truth," in Langer's phrase?[6]

While history of the Holocaust must be read and taught, it should not, and it could not, be the sole source for one's knowledge and understanding of the Holocaust. For the mere factual truth does not, by itself, involve the reader emotionally and intellectually. For most human beings the very magnitude of the Holocaust is beyond comprehension; thus, there might be an attempt to reject or suppress it. The mere use of facts may resemble the use of other historical facts, and thus may diminish the uniqueness of this terrible event in the annals of mankind. Factual information may lack the ethical ramifications of the Shoah (the Holocaust), and may not touch the readers or involve them emotionally. Numbers alone tend to obfuscate the meaning of the Holocaust.

As one protagonist in Yehuda Amichai's Holocaust novel *Not of This Time, Not of This Place*, which will be discussed in an ensuing chapter, says: "History will describe the event [...]: 'So-and-so many Jews and Germans were killed in the great war.' Here will be a balancing and equalizing of oppressed and oppressors."[7]

---

6. Langer, *The Holocaust and the Literary Imagination*, p. 8.
7. Yehuda Amicahi, *Not of This Time, Not of This Place* (New York, 1968),

In order to overcome this shortcoming, the use of imaginative writing is suggested. A work of literary art, asserted the critic Richard Gilman, "inoculates history with a serum of invented insights which actually immunize the reader against mere factual truths and force him into a more painful confrontation with the implications about himself and his world that this serum sends coursing through his emotional and intellectual bloodstream."[8]

Indeed, Gilman concluded, "literature, like all art, is the account of what history has failed to produce on its own."[9]

Are documentary writings on the Holocaust considered to be in the domain of history? Sidra DeKoven Ezrahi suggested that some documentary writings are not necessarily 'factual' or historical. She argued that "Documentary art is a hybrid genre between fact and fiction." It employs creative imagination to point out some transcendental significance of the historical processes.[10]

It is that unique impact of artistic literature on the reader which ought to be mentioned in this context. It is not information that is conveyed in literary works of art, but rather the very human experience. Through prose and poetry writing on the Holocaust, the reader is made to undergo some aspect of the experience of the Holocaust. While not physically involved, the reader is indeed emotionally and intellectually involved – in as much as it is possible – with past experiences of other human beings.

Through the use of artistic devices by a Holocaust writer, the reader is given access to perception and insight into the events of the Holocaust and their meaning. He is able to grasp the essence of the Holocaust and learn about its implication to Jews and to humanity in general. He may get some extraordinary insights into the unique meaning of this calamity that killed one half of the Jewish people and millions of other people. The reader may thus gain some understanding of what brought a so-called civilized nation, at the height of its achievements in science, art, and culture, to an abyss never before imagined or experienced by human beings.

Through the reading of *belles lettres* on the Holocaust, the sensitive reader may be further aware of the potential danger to humanity from man himself. This literature may crystallize some current events, even in remote parts of the globe, in light of the Holocaust.

---

p. 295.

8.   As cited by Langer, *The Holocaust and the Literary Imagination*, p. 8. This quotation is not found in Gilman's article cited in note 9.

9.   Richard Gilman, "Nat Turner Revisited," *The New Republic*, 158 (No. 17, April 27, 1968); see also Langer, *The Holocaust and the Literary Imagination*, p. 8.

10.   Sidra DeKoven Ezrahi, *By Words Alone* (Chicago & London, 1979), p. 23.

Each and every writer under study is unique, and his artistic way in relating the experience of the Holocaust, its concept and perception, may differ from those of other Holocaust writers, as expounded in the ensuing chapters. Nevertheless, they all have one thing in common: an attempt to present the Holocaust experience, its background and its aftermath in an artistic way through literature.

•

The first part of the book deals with prose writers who told the experience of the Holocaust from within. Namely, they are Jewish survivors, writing about the Holocaust either in Hebrew or in a Western language.

The second part of the book examines Hebrew writers who wrote about the Holocaust after the war, addressing the experience and its aftermarth from without.

All works discussed in the book have been translated into English.

Holocaust Literature in Criticism

Critics of literature have hesitated for a long time to discuss literary works concerning the Holocaust on their literary merits or to consider them as a special genre, now referred to as Holocaust literature or literature of atrocity. While sporadic reviews did appear in connection with the publication of literary works on the Holocaust, more comprehensive evaluation on the literary value of such works have been a phenomenon that began 25 years after World War II.

In the 1970s, one notes the publication of several book-long works of criticism on the literature of the Holocaust. Irving Halperin published his book titled *Messengers from the Dead* in 1970,[11] which contains, among other things, a discussion of Elie Wiesel's works. A more definitive literary discussion and a more impressive treatment of literature of atrocity as a special form of literature was offered in 1975 by Lawrence Langer in his *The Holocaust and the Literary Imagination*, which has been cited before. This book and Langer's subsequent works have had a seminal influence on literary criticism of Holocaust literature.[12]

---

11. Irving Halperin, *Messengers from the Dead* (Philadelphia, 1970).

12. Langer, *The Holocaust and the Literary Imagination* (full citation in note 2). Langer followed this work with his book *The Age of Atrocity* (Boston, 1978) on the theme of death in modern literature. He continued his pursuit of Holocaust literature with *Versions of Survival, The Holocaust and the Human Spirit* (Albany, 1982), and *Preempting the Holocaust* (New Haven, 1998), and others. Several articles published in the 1970s reviewed Langer's work, and are indicative of growing interest in this subject matter; they are, among others: Edward Alexander, "The Holocaust in American Jewish Fiction: A Slow Awakening," *Judaism*, XXV (No. 3, Summer 1976), pp. 320–330; Norma Rosen, "The Holocaust and the American Jewish Novelist," *Midstream*, XX (No. 8, October 1974), pp. 54–62;

In the late 1970s and 1980s, there was a surge of books of literary criticism on Holocaust literature. Edward Alexander published his *The Resonance of Dust* (1979), in which he examined a Holocaust diary by Moshe Flinker, Jewish and Hebrew poetry by Nelly Sachs and Abba Kovner, and Hebrew prose by Yehuda Amichai, Hanoch Bartov, Hayim Gouri, and others, some of whom are discussed in the following chapters.[13] Two significant contributions to the field were published by Sidra DeKoven Ezrahi, *By Words Alone* (1979), and by Alvin Rosenfeld, *A Double Dying* (1980).[14]

In 1984, two books presented a wider scope by addressing the responses to catastrophe in Hebrew and Jewish literature. David Roskies examined "Responses to Catastrophe in Modern Jewish Culture," from the early liturgy to contemporary Yiddish literature, in his *Against the Apocalypse.*[15] And Alan Mintz probed "Responses to Catastrophe in Hebrew Literature," from lamentations to Midrash, from medieval literature to contemporary Hebrew letters, in his book *Hurban: Responses to Catastrophe in Hebrew Literature.* Mintz studied such Hebrew poets and prose writers as Uri Zvi Greenberg, Aharon Appelfeld, Hanoch Bartov, Hayim Gouri, and Yehuda Amichai.[16]

An observer of Holocaust-related works of criticism may note the abundance of books, in addition to numerous articles, on Elie Wiesel, which were published before and after he was awarded the Nobel Peace Prize in 1986. Among the many works, it is worthwhile mentioning, in the context of studies on Holocaust literature, the collection of essays on Wiesel titled *Confronting the Holocaust: The Impact of Elie Wiesel* (1978), edited by Alvin Rosenfeld and Irving Greenberg, and Ellen Fine's *Legacy of Night, The Literary Universe of Elie Wiesel* (1982).[17]

Concurrently, a number of critics concentrated on the Holocaust theme as found in American Jewish fiction (Alan Berger; Arthur Cohen), in women's literature (Marlene L. Heinemann), or in art (Stephen Lewis).[18]

David Stern, "Imagining the Holocaust," *Commentary*, 62 (No. 1, July 1976), pp. 46–51.

13. Edward Alexander, *The Resonance of Dust* (Columbus, 1979).

14. DeKoven Ezrahi, *By Words Alone* (full citation in note 10); Rosenfeld, *A Double Dying: Reflections on Holocaust Literature* (full citation in note 5). See also Rosenfeld's *Imagining Hitler* (Bloomington, 1985).

15. David G. Roskies, *Against the Apocalypse: Responses to Catastrophe in Modern Jewish Culture* (Cambridge, 1984).

16. Alan L. Mintz, *Hurban: Responses to Catastrophe in Hebrew Literature* (New York, 1984).

17. Alvin H. Rosenfeld & Irving Greenberg, ed., *Confronting the Holocaust: The Impact of Elie Wiesel* (Bloomington, 1978); Ellen Fine, *Legacy of Night, The Literary Universe of Elie Wiesel* (Albany, 1982).

18. Alan L. Berger, *Crisis and Covenant: The Holocaust in American Jewish Fiction* (Albany, 1985); see also Edward Alexander's article cited in note 12 above; Arthur Allen Cohen, *The American Imagination After the War: Notes on the Novel, Jews and Hope* (Syracuse, 1981); Marlene L. Heinemann, *Gender and Destiny:*

The limited discussion of Holocaust literature written in Hebrew is quite noticeable. Apart from several chapters or articles written by such critics as Robert Alter, Gershon Shaked, and Leon Yudkin, very little has been published in English during the 1960s and 1970s on the Holocaust as portrayed in modern Hebrew letters.[19]

The 1980s marked a significant increase of books published on the theme of the Holocaust in modern Hebrew literature with Murray J. Kohn's book *The Voice of My Blood Cries Out* (1979) on Hebrew poetry, and Alan J. Yuter's *The Holocaust in Hebrew Literature* (1983). Yuter examined Ka-tzetnik briefly, but did not analyze the book under study in the chapter on Ka-tzetnik in this book. Another work published in the 1980s is an anthology of Israeli fiction, *Facing the Holocaust*, with an introduction by Gila Ramras-Rauch and afterword by Gershon Shaked.[20] Ramras-Rauch also published a book on Appelfeld in 1994.[21] James Young dealt with representation of the Holocaust in documentaries, memoirs, cinema, and theater in his *Writing and Rewriting the Holocaust* (1990).[22]

One may note that even in Israel very little has been published on the literary aspects of Holocaust literature, with the exception of numerous reviews and books of Aharon Appelfeld's prose, although several anthologies of texts and analysis were published in the 1970s.[23]

Women Writers on the Holocaust (Westport, 1986); Stephen Lewis, *Art Out of Agony, The Holocaust Theme in Literature, Sculpture and Film* (Montreal & New York, 1984), which contains a conversation with Aharon Appelfeld.

19. Robert Alter, *After the Tradition* (New York, 1960); Gershon Shaked, "Childhood Lost: Studies in the Holocaust Themes in Contemporary Israel Fiction," *Literature East and West*, XIV (No. 1, March 1970), pp. 90–108; Leon I. Yudkin, *Escape into Siege* (London & Boston, 1974). See also Alexander's book cited in note 13 above.

20. Murray J. Kohn, *The Voice of My Blood Cries Out* (New York, 1979); Alan J. Yuter, *The Holocaust in Hebrew Literature, From Genocide to Rebirth* (Port Washington, N.Y., 1983), which has chapters on Ka-tzetnik, Kaniuk, Kovner, Greenberg, Pagis, Carmi, Appelfeld, Ben Amotz, Amichai, Bartov, Oz, Shenhar, Hazaz, and Agnon; Gila Ramras-Rauch and Joseph Michman-Melkman, ed., *Facing the Holocaust: Selected Israeli Fiction*, with an introduction by G. Ramras-Rauch and afterword by Gershon Shaked (Philadelphia, 1985). See also Mintz's book cited in note 16 above.

21. Gila Ramras-Rauch, *Aharon Appelfeld: The Holocaust and Beyond* (Bloomington, 1994).

22. James E. Young, *Writing and Rewriting the Holocaust* (Bloomington, 1990).

23. Some of them are: Natan Gross, Itamar Yaoz-Kest and Rina Klinov, ed., *Hashoah Bashirah Ha'ivrit* [Holocaust in Hebrew Poetry], with an introduction by Hillel Barzel (Tel Aviv, 1974) [Hebrew]; Shammai Golan, ed., *Hashoah, Pirkei Edut Vesifrut* [The Holocaust: Eye Witness and Literary Accounts] (Tel Aviv, 1976) [Hebrew]. And recently, books on individual writers such as Aharon Appelfeld by Yigal Schwartz, *Individual Lament and Tribal Eternity* (Jerusalem, 1996) [Hebrew].

While many aspects of the literary study and critical analysis about non-Hebraic works do indeed pertain to works originally written in Hebrew, there are some unique features in Hebrew literature which merit the attention of any student of the literary expression of the Holocaust experience.

They are discussed in the following chapters.

The Holocaust Experience
From Within

Chapter 1
Aharon Appelfeld: Premonition and Illusion in the Pre-Holocaust Years in *Badenheim 1939*

Aharon Appelfeld is one of the few Jewish writers who continue to ponder endlessly in their writing about the terrible riddle of the Holocaust phenomena and its experience. In a tenacious and diligent manner, he goes on to create and recreate, in his uniquely artistic way, the terrible experiences that the survivors of the Holocaust went through during and after the war. In like manner, he delineates the pre-Holocaust reality in Europe.

His protagonists pass very close to the sites of the Holocaust and near the terrible events, but very seldom do they come to the very locales where the atrocities have been perpetrated. Appelfeld is at his best in creating the atmosphere of the Shoah and in describing the psychological and spiritual impact on the individual Jew as an individual and as part of Jewish society.

Appelfeld's stories and novels which were initially written and published in Hebrew have been translated into English, and have been published in the U.S. and Europe in the past twenty-five years. Some of his early short stories have been translated into English and published in various periodicals. A collection of his short stories was published in Israel under the title *In the Wilderness* (1965), but apparently did not get a wide circulation. One of his early works, a novella titled *Badenheim 1939*[1] that has been translated into English and was published in 1980 in an abridged form, was originally

---

1. Aharon Appelfeld, *Badenheim 1939* (Boston: David R. Godine, 1980; New York: Washington Square Press, 1981), translated by Dalia Bilu. Aharon Appelfeld, *In the Wilderness: Stories* (Jerusalem: Achshav Publishing House, 1965). In the following citations of the text in parentheses the first page number refers to the Boston edition while the second page number refers to the New York edition.

published in Hebrew five years earlier under the title "Badenheim, a Resort City."[2] This novella is the subject of this chapter as typical of Appelfeld's literary art.

As the English title indicates, the story takes place in 1939, and it is probably before the beginning of the war. Appelfeld recreates a reality of assimilated Jews in a resort town, where mysterious signs of some foreboding calamity are increasingly emerging.

The reader, who of course is knowledgeable about the Shoah, is indeed very sensitive to the signs and to the proverbial handwriting on the wall. However, Appelfeld's characters do not notice the alarming signs and the messages that they send. The vacationers in Badenheim continue to enjoy the luxuries and the delicacies that the resort town has to offer and continue to indulge in the German-Austrian culture. They devour sumptuous cakes, lick pink ice cream, and soar on the wings of lofty music.

The structure of the novel follows the well established historical phenomena that most people at that time failed to interpret the signs of a pending calamity. It is some sort of a myopia that characterized not only European Jewry but also most of the world concerning the lurking threat to annihilate the Jewish people.

This psychological propensity was coupled with similar attitude even when the information about the Nazis' acts of killing and destruction was known in political and diplomatic circles by persons who could have acted to save the Jews. They did not believe or did not want to believe the reports (as proven in various historical studies).

Even among survivors of the Holocaust and those who witnessed the atrocities one often hears the statement: "I could not believe my eyes," a statement that has been documented in the literature in Elie Wiesel's *Night*[3] and in interviews with survivors.[4]

Yet the reader is fully aware of the meaning of various signs and signals, and correctly reads the handwriting on the wall based on his post-Holocaust knowledge. Having an advantage over the protagonists, the reader is thus placed in a very interesting position and is fully involved in the story. The reader is aware of the consequences of the war and wishes he could alert the easy-going, unsuspecting protagonists of the pending disaster.

---

2. Aharon Appelfeld, "Badenheim, Ir Nofesh" [Badenheim, a Resort Town], *Shanim Vesha'ot* [Years and Hours] (Israel, 1975), pp. 5–103 [Hebrew].

3. Elie Wiesel, *Night* (New York: Avon Books, 1969), p. 42: "I could not believe it."

4. In a TV program named "Kitie," a testimony of a survivor who visited Auschwitz with her son, aired in channel 13 in New York on February 4, 1981, she testified that she did not, or could not, "believe her eyes."

Exposition: Landscape and Season as Metaphors

As in many of Appelfeld's other stories, his depiction of landscape alludes to the pending calamity and functions as a foreshadowing of events that are to take place. The story opens with a spring-like statement: "Spring returned to Badenheim" (p. 1; 7). Through the play of light and shadow the narrator displays a semblance of some lighting: "The shadows of the forest retreated to the trees. The sun scattered the remnants of the darkness and its light filled the main street" (p. 1; 7).

This exposition, intended to instill a feeling of light and warmth and the changing seasons, is somewhat misleading, for the forest – that Gothic representation of German's past – remains in the backdrop and will continue to cast its menacing shadows later on. Immediately after the description of the returning spring, the narrator presents an evaluative summary: "It was a moment of transition" (p. 1; 7). This is a loaded statement that may be read on two levels. It may be related to the change of seasons, mentioned before, or to another level of perception altogether.

And indeed this kind of dual meaning in loaded phrases abounds in many of Appelfeld's stories. These loaded phrases extend their message beyond the mere level of landscape description to more meaningful levels of interpretation. The recurrence of such utterances and their integration into the descriptions of landscape and people intensify these statements and extend the story beyond its overt level of storytelling.

The first encounter with this literary device occurs in the description of Trude, the sickly wife of the pharmacist (an incongruity created by placing illness in the proximity of healing). As if through her unique perspective, the narrator recalls the hard winter that came on the city: "A strange, hard winter. Storms had swept through the town" (p. 1; 7), and concurrently the narrator interjects, as if in the thoughts of the sickly woman, "Rumors were rife" – a phrase that continues the movement of the violent actions of nature ("... and torn the roofs off the houses," p. 1; 7), but coupled with the adjective "strange" transcends the mere depiction of landscape to the sphere of human relations.

This depiction of stormy nature and the loaded phrases are related for they form a bond of continuity and reciprocity. Thus Appelfeld creates an air of desolation, perhaps some sort of "an apocalyptical fear" that he has referred to in his book of essays.[5] Unidentified fears, Kafkaesque in some respect, lurk in the air of the novel's reality. Appelfeld's continuous use of this device will be discussed below.

---

5. Aharon Appelfeld, *Masot Beguf Rishon* [Essays in First Person] (Jerusalem, 1979), p. 22 [Hebrew].

The Sanitation Department and Its Role

While the narrator relates how the Jewish vacationers get ready for the music festival which takes place during this vacation season in Badenheim, and as he describes the orchestra players and the impresario, Dr. Pappenheim, all Jews, there occurs a "moment of transition" in the town itself.

It happens as the municipal Department of Sanitation suddenly gets mysterious authority, some 'extended jurisdiction,' "to conduct independent investigations [...] the inspectors spread out and [...] began investigating" (p. 11; 19). Yet, no one knew what they were investigating. Consequently, "Rumors were rife" again. Some of the vacationers attributed the inspectors' investigations to an attempt to locate "a health hazard," while others thought that the inspectors were in effect "Income Tax collectors in disguise" (p. 12; 20). Thus, there is some mystery about the 'investigations' and an ambiguity as to the actual role and meaning of the Sanitation Department. Subsequently, it appears that all citizens who are Jewish have to register with the Sanitation Department (p. 20; 32).

What is the meaning of such an act? Obviously, it is the narrator's way of raising the issue of Jewish identity, which these mostly assimilated Jews are attempting to ignore or suppress. Now, these Jews are required to identify themselves as Jews, something that they did not bother to do previously, having been 'liberated' from the shackles of their Jewish background in the post-Enlightenment society of Europe. Appelfeld then recreates the conditions that occurred in Nazi Germany in the 1930s, when such a requirement was enforced on Jews, whether they were whole Jews or *Mischlinge* (of mixed race). It is this actual decree that occurred before 1939 which is given a literary setting in the novella with the added metaphor of the Sanitation Department.

Faced with this requirement, the naive reaction of these Jews is reproduced by the narrator. Dr. Pappenheim rationalizes that apparently the Sanitation Department wants to show pride in its important guests, and plans to write their names in its 'Golden Book,' resembling a 'hall of fame' recognition. "Isn't that handsome of them?" is his summation (p. 23; 34). Mrs. Zauberblit praises the department for its "order and beauty" (p. 24; 36).

The activities of the Sanitation Department are further expanded by additional information provided by the narrator. "In the Sanitation Department they knew everything [...] and they were glad to show a man his past" (p. 38; 53). The department undertakes to probe the ancestral background of these assimilated Jews regardless of their efforts, successful and otherwise, to assimilate into their surrounding society. It does not take into consideration such trivialities as the fact that Frau Zauberblit was half Jewish and had a 'nobility' background, having been the mistress of a Graf. And of course her name, which ironically means in Yiddish that she is of 'clean blood,' does not help either. The German meaning implies something 'megical' (Zauber) about her. The assimilationists may reject their Jewish background and may even exhibit self-hatred, saying, as one does, "You must admit that the Jews are an ugly people. I can't see that they're any use to anyone" (p. 72; 92). But expressing this attitude toward Jews and Judaism does not help them.

The identity of the Sanitation Department is intentionally vague and its role is purposefully ambiguous, even though its dealings with extended questions of property ownership, inheritance, registration, etc., by the inspectors (pp. 11–12; 19–20) begin to provide clearer clues to the reader as to what it is. The metaphor aspect created with the Sanitation Department – beyond its routine duties of clearing refuse – becomes clear to the reader. However, the meaning and significance are totally oblivious to the Jewish vacationers in Badenheim in 1939.

Interjecting Foreboding Warning

The narrator continues to create an air of melancholy and depression not only through the landscape, as mentioned above, but also by interjecting those dual meaning phrases such as, "A secret worry crept over the faces of the aging musicians" (p. 12; 20); "rumors were rife" (p. 12; 20); "And the investigations showed what reality was. [...] Estrangement, suspicion, and mistrust began to invade the town. But the people were still preoccupied with their own affairs" (pp. 19–20; 31). These statements imply a point of view and a frame of reference which are farther from 1939. Definitely they belong to the post-Holocaust era as attested to by an editorial comment of a single word supplemented by the narrator ("still..."). The narrator contributes a clearer statement later, in a comment using the same adverb: "it still seemed that some other time, from some other place, had invaded the town and was silently establishing itself" (p. 38; 54).

The narrator presents a continuous and gradual revelation of additional clues through the plot of the story as the novel unfolds: the town is being closed down; no one comes in or goes out. He continues to employ objects taken from the context of the Holocaust that are loaded with important symbolism, such as the fences that the inspectors build with the evocative barbed wire and the cement pillars. These are objects which the reader in the post-Holocaust age can identify clearly as alluding to the experience of the Holocaust and thus to a lurking calamity. Yet the explanation offered by the narrator, which is supposed to reflect the mentality and the naïveté of most Jewish people at the time, is that these were "suggestive of preparations for a public celebration" (p. 15; 23).

The narrator continues to provide additional clues as the plot develops, such as the possibility that the vacationers will be returning to Poland where some of them were born. (p. 52; 69). Also, there are further developments within the town; it appears as though it is under siege. The town is totally isolated from the rest of the world, apparently "in quarantine" (p. 71; 91), a term that is loaded with allusion to the Shoah and to the Nazis' early stages of ghettoization of the Jews from the Arian population. Another metaphor used in this conjunction is the 'plague' (see below).

Additional clues of the pending calamity are placed by the narrator in protagonists' mouths as they use certain words which, unknowingly to them, extend beyond their timely context. While these speakers do not comprehend the urgent messages imbedded in what they say, the meanings are noticeable by the reader. This use of the narrator to implant ironical information goes beyond the concept of the unreliable narrator – the narrator who provides the reader with information that is 'false,' or unreliable. Here the narrator provides true information that has an extended meaning. This is a very clever way of manipulating the narrator's voice so as to reflect the authentic predilection of people at that time. Thus, Dr. Pappenheim, distraught that Mandelbaum does show up for the festival, summarizes the situation as "A catastrophe" (p. 19; 28), which in effect foreshadows the terrible events that are about to occur. He does not know what he is saying, but the reader gets the message. The irony is that his 'catastrophe' is dwarfed by that major catastrophe which is about to take place.

Similarly, even a trivial side-story may at times allude to the pending catastrophe, using, naively but intentionally, the language of the Shoah. The headwaiter tells one of the guests about "the terrible catastrophe" that had taken place in the aquarium the year before when blue Cambium fish were put together with the other fish, and "one night they suddenly fell on the other fish and massacred them horribly," and in the morning "the floor of the aquarium was full of corpses" (p. 51; 66).

Appelfeld provides additional clues of various steps leading to the Holocaust. The Sanitation Department has closed the water supply (p. 47; 63); then the telephones went dead (p. 70; 90), and the post office was closed (pp. 70–71; 90–91). All means of communications were cut off. The handwriting was on the wall, and most people did notice it: the maids "had flown as if the houses were on fire" (p. 70; 90), but the Jews could not go anywhere and could not do anything at this point.

The narrator uses flashback to send a relevant message that is understood in the context of the Holocaust. He relates that a few years earlier a strange person has appeared in the town who was shouting at the passers-by, "Save your souls while there is still time!" (p. 41; 57).

The people's illusion and inability to see the signs and accurately interpret them are exemplified by some of the protagonists. For example, Frau Zauberblit comments rather naively on the activities of the Sanitation Department, "Everything's going according to plan. Isn't it wonderful?" (p.

35; 51). It is of course a loaded statement, identified as such by the reader who is aware of the history of the Shoah.

Trude: Apocalyptic Sense of Destruction

In Appelfeld's stories women play an important role through their sensitivities that at times are excessively morbid, yet they carry within them the bitter truth that others do not see nor sense. In portraying his protagonists in *Badenheim 1939*, Appelfeld assigns a special role to an apocalyptic figure of a woman, Trude, who evokes a prophetic sense of foreboding and destruction. Trude is hallucinating about the fate of her daughter, suspecting that her husband beats her (p. 3; 8). Through her hyper-sensitivities, Appelfeld portrays Trude as foreshadowing a foreboding sense of calamity while everybody else is enjoying life and devouring "pink ice cream" (p. 2; 8). Through her unique perception, the reader gets a glimpse of the guests who are coming to Badenheim: "To Trude they looked not like the familiar vacationers, but like patients in a sanitarium" (p. 3; 9). Appelfeld has her say directly that "They look very pale." Expanding her view, the narrator reports that to her, "The whole world looked transparent" for indeed "It was poisoned and diseased" (p. 3; 9).

Trude's role is intensified as she is rousing the street with her screams, but no one pays attention to her (prophetic?) warning (p. 25; 36). Appelfeld hints that her hallucinations and warnings transcend normal reality as she sees into events about to take place. Applefeld uses imagery in her husband's words. As he tries to calm her, Martin says, "Calm yourself, Trude, calm yourself. There's no forest here. There are no wolves here" (p. 25; 36).

The reference to 'wolves' and to the 'forest' – the latter appearing in the beginning of the novel – is intensified by the child singer. This child prodigy, who is part of the musical troupe, is singing "about the dark forest where the wolf dwelt" (p. 46; 62). Thus, the metaphoric 'forest' whose shadows retreated in the beginning of the novel comes back now to haunt the Jewish vacationers.

Women's Illness

Women's morbid sensitivity here, as well as in Appelfeld's other stories (see "Bertha," "Regina"),[6] and their illness, whether before the Holocaust or afterwards, foreshadow the lurking illness that is about to infect the spouse or the males in the group, and in this story, the rest of the Jewish vacationers. In his stories, male protagonists are characterized as attempting to ignore the illness and even deny its existence, especially in stories that depict survivors

---

6. Aharon Appelfeld, "Bertha," in *Facing the Holocaust*, Gila Ramras-Rauch, Joseph Michman-Melkman, ed. (Philadelphia, 1985), pp. 143–159.

after the war. However, at the end of their psychological, spiritual, and physical struggle, these male protagonists, too, succumb to the sickness, very much like their wives or women friends. Some of these women represent a suppressed mirror image of the world of the Holocaust and its experience in which survivors are attempting to ignore and reject as part of their post-Holocaust desire to live a semblance of a normal life (such as in the story "Bertha").

Appelfeld alludes to this notion throughout this novel. In the beginning of the story, as the menacing shadows are seen through Trude's eyes, the narrator reveals that "Trude's illness seeped into his soul drop by drop. Her husband too began to see patches of paleness on people's faces" (pp. 3–4; 9), and consequently, he "felt that he was becoming infected by her hallucinations" (p. 11; 17).

Trude is different than most of the other protagonists in the attachment to her Jewish parents and thus to her Jewish heritage. The narrator provides the following information through her husband's perception: "Trude was always talking about her parents [...]. Her parents were dead" (p. 10; 17). The meaning of her attachment is also provided through her husband, who says "that she was still stuck in that world, in the mountains among the Jews" (p. 10; 17). And the narrator, in his role as an omniscient narrator who presents the story with his guiding clues, assures the reader that "in a sense, he was right." Trude's role is to express her premonition, based on an unconscious, deeply rooted existential apprehension, for "She was haunted by a hidden fear, not her own" (pp. 10–11; 17).

Illness as a Central Metaphor

Illness is one of the central metaphors of the novel. It is not only Trude, identified with some Jewish heritage, who is inflicted with an inexplicable illness. Not only is illness viewed from her perspective, most of the characters in the novel, whether assimilated or not, are described from various points of view as having some kind of an illness.

From the townspeople's perspective, the foreigners "had insinuated themselves like diseased roots" (p. 4; 10).[7] The weird twin brothers who recited poetry as part of their performace had a "morbid melody throbbing in their voices" (p. 17; 27); "it was as if their sickness had two voices" (p. 18; 27). Their "morbid voices" touched Samitzky's "infected cells," according to his own statement (p. 18; 28). Mandelbaum "had been taken ill" and could not keep his engagement (p. 19; 28), and "people began avoiding Dr. Pappenheim like the plague" (p. 21; 32).

---

7.   The original Hebrew has it: "who have planted themselves like diseased roots" (Appelfeld, "Bedenheim Ir Nofesh," p. 9) [Hebrew].

The meaning of this symbolic sickness becomes more apparent later, as the narrator enhances the metaphor, saying, "People began unburdening themselves to each other as if they were speaking of an old illness which there was no longer any point in hiding, and their reactions were different: shame and pride" (p. 21; 32). Additional revelations about the nature of the illness abound as it is related that "Trude's illness had grown worse. She spoke about death all the time, no longer in fear but with a kind of intimacy" (p. 21; 32). People at the hotel spoke of the twins "as invalids" (p. 24; 35).[8] And indeed, some of the others seem to be sick as well: Frau Zauberblit has a temperature and is in pain (p. 62; 81). Dr. Pappenheim defines the 'illness' as "A Jewish epidemic" (p. 71; 91). The rabbi, representing Judaism, too, is inflicted with a "paralytic stroke" (p. 100; 125).

This multi-faceted presentation which has a multiplicity of points of view forms the metaphor of the sickness as a unique phenomenon that typified Jewish reality in Europe before the war. It has an historiosophic concept which extends beyond the confines of the novel and attempts to make a comment on an existential level about the pre-war condition and mentality of European Jewry. Both traditional and assimilated Jews in Europe are portrayed on two levels of perception: one that recreates the naïveté of pre-war Jews, and another – more sophisticated and clandestine – that assumes the point of view and knowledge of a survivor who had witnessed the atrocities and had experienced the horrors of the Holocaust. To the survivor, European Jewry before the war appears to be a Jewry in decline, a sickly Jewry, either paralyzed or at a slumber, which is forced despite its resentment – especially the assimilated – to return to its origins. In his essays, Appelfeld refers to this condition as "the deterioration of faith and ideas."[9]

Upon their forced return to Poland, which seems to be a returning that is also some type of repentance,[10] the rabbi mutters:

What do they want? All these years they haven't paid any attention to the Torah. Me they locked away in an old-age home. They didn't want to have anything to do with me. Now they want to go to Poland. There is no atonement [repentance] without seeking forgiveness first (p. 143; 171).

The answer (the Hebrew *teshuvah*, meaning also repenting) does not come.

In summary, it is with great artistic intensity that Appelfeld has created a pre-Holocaust reality reflecting the actual Holocaust reality which is about to take place. The death machine is getting ready and the execution of the early

---

8.   Original Hebrew: "as sick people," *ibid.*, p. 22 [Hebrew].

9.   In his essays, in which he refers to the war and its aftermath; Appelfeld, *Masot Beguf Rishon*, p. 22 [Hebrew].

10.   The Hebrew *shiva*, meaning return, has the same root as *teshuvah*, meaning repenting.

stages of the Holocaust, starting with checking identity, seclusion and concentration, and finally, in our novel, the deportation. The transport train at the end of the novel is the very beginning of the historical Holocaust.

Appelfeld has created a 'dictionary' of terms, so to speak, that endeavors to recreate the unfathomable mental condition of the Jewish vacationers in a pre-war Austrian town. Everything in the story leads to the coming catastrophe, but no one can read the proverbial handwriting on the wall.

Even as the people are being transported in the "filthy freight" train, the psychological defense mechanism, or the self delusion, still functions. The narrator has Dr. Peppenhein say the final words in the novel: "If the couches are so dirty it must mean that we have not far to go" (p. 148; 175).

Chapter 2
Elie Wiesel: the *Night* of Auschwitz –
The Right to Question

Elie Wiesel is the great questioner among writers of Holocaust literature. Needless to say, he has not been the first author, or among the first, who undertook to describe the Holocaust experience through the art of literature. There were other writers before him. However, more than any other writer in the Western world, it has been Wiesel's writings that aroused the conscience of the enlightened world anew and demanded that the Holocaust phenomenon be addressed honestly and openly some twenty years after the end of World War II.

Elie Wiesel's impact as a writer and as a humanist has been recognized for years and acknowledged by the Nobel Peace Prize, which was awarded him in 1986. His contribution to literature and to the awareness of the Holocaust has been attested to in his numerous books and articles. Relentlessly, Wiesel continues to remind the world about the past and to alert humanity against genocides and inequities as an advocate of human rights in the present.

This chapter aims to discuss and analyze Wiesel's literary art as evidenced in his semi-autobiographical story, *Night*.[1]

•

As the great questioner in the literature of the Holocaust, Wiesel poses potential questions to mankind and to God, questions that we all ask in our heart: "How could the Holocaust happen? What is its meaning to humanity? And – the faithful will add – where was God?"

---

1. Elie Wiesel, *Night* (New York: Avon Books, 1969); Elie Wiesel, *Night* (New York: Bantam Books, 1982). Citations in parentheses in the text will refer first to the Avon edition and then to the Bantam edition. In referring to *Night* I will use the term *story*, not *novel*, to exclude any notion that it is a work of fiction.

Wiesel's art in *Night* is exemplified in his masterly and authentic depiction of the death camp experience, and, moreover, by his ability to address the unique significance of the Holocaust in the annals of mankind and its meaning in the history of the Jewish people. Despite several weaknesses that some critics such as A. Alvarez have found in his style and in his craftsmanship,[2] Wiesel's achievement as a writer, and especially as a Holocaust writer, is anchored in his ability to weave the fabric of the story around central existential themes that reach to the very depth of the Holocaust phenomenon. These themes leave an ineradicable impact on the reader who is compelled to experience the Holocaust in the only possible way – as an outside observer.

The Question Mark

Wiesel sets the question at the base of *Night*'s intrinsic structure. The critics Irving Halpern and Lawrence Langer recognized the existence of the question in Wiesel's writings, but neither has identified the centrality of the question in the structure of *Night* and its role in the story.[3]

The centrality of the question in the reality of the Holocaust as conceptualized by the narrator appears at the beginning of the story in the characterization of Moché the Beadle.[4] Moché is depicted as elevating the question to an existential sphere of reference. A man of God in the story, Moché teaches Eliezer, the story's protagonist, that "Man raises himself toward God by the questions he asks Him" (*Night*, p. 14, Avon edition; p. 2, Bantam edition). According to this relationship between man and God, "Man questions God and God answers," but apparently man does not understand God's answer. Moché explains, "You will find the true answers, Eliezer, only within yourself" (p. 14; 3). Thus, Wiesel artistically builds up the instrinsic structure of his story in preparation for the eminent questions posed by Wiesel, the author, and Eliezer, his autobiographical protagonist.

The question mark is characteristic of the narrator's point of view; it keeps recurring throughout, setting the dominant tone of the story. The questions are asked from various points of view and are used to convey several messages. At times the narrator voices questions echoing questions that were

---

2. A. Alvarez, "The Literature of the Holocaust," *Beyond All This Fiddle* [:] Essays 1955-1967 (New York, 1968), p. 23: "As a human document, *Night* is almost unbearably painful, and certainly beyond criticism. But [...] it is a failure as a work of art [...] Wiesel [...] falls back on rhetoric...."
3. Irving Halperin, *Messengers from the Dead* (Philadelphia, 1970), pp. 70, 72, etc.; Lawrence L. Langer, *The Holocaust and the Literary Imagination* (New Haven, 1975), p. 79.
4. The name Moché is spelled the French way; in some editions his name is spelled Moshe.

apparently asked by Jews before the Holocaust, such as, "Was he [Hitler] going to wipe out a whole people?" (p. 17; 6). Another set of questions reflects a different stand – that of retrospection. It is the view of the author who finds himself already beyond the experience of the Holocaust and its horrible outcome and tries to return to its very experience, but is unable to throw off the knowledge of its aftermath.

The narrator's use of retrospection is multi-faceted. He is not only relating the past by way of a condensed summary or through scenes and dialogues. The narrator shifts from a narrative of events in progress to an evaluation, which is in effect a retrospective assessment based on hindsight and personal experience of that event that occurred in the past. Thus, the narrator exclaims, "Yes, we even doubted that he [Hitler] wanted to exterminate us" (p. 17; 6), with the exclamatory interjection 'yes' and the editorial adverb 'even.'

The questions are directed at the reader and demand meaningful contemporary answers. This is how Wiesel molds the internal message of his story – in a manner that permeates unwittingly to the reader. As he asks the questions, the narrator is an omniscient narrator, using the tone of irony, he implies – as other authors did – that the Jews did not recognize the pre-Holocaust signs, the handwriting on the wall, and if they did, they interpreted the signs naively. Thus, Wiesel has created a complex structure of the narrator's point of view, adding a dimension to his role in the story. By pointing out the 'blind spot' of Jews who did not understand the political and social situation correctly in time, the author is signaling to his contemporary reader to be alert to present-day signs of lurking dangers of any major social catastrophe. In this way, the relevance of the Holocaust and its message is made meaningful to contemporary people in general and to Jews in particular.

Flow of Time

A unique feature in *Night* which is advanced by the author is the perception of time. In order to relay a different treatment of the passage of time in Holocaust writing, the narrator does not try to impart to the reader any sense of progress in time. On the contrary, the conventional patterns of time are shattered by the presentation of the Holocaust reality not just as events occurring in the past, but as events that project to the future. It is done through intertwining information acquired only after the war into the narrative of the past. An example for such use may be found in the episode of the knocking that they heard on the boarded windows of their home. Only after the war does the first-person narrator learn that it was the police inspector, his father's friend, who could have saved them (pp. 23–24; 12) In this manner, the author creates tension between the story as it occurred and as it could have occurred. In addition, there is also a sense of irony that emerges out of knowing future events 'in advance.' The reader is required to reach conclusions and is made to engage in the "if/then" mold of thinking, namely, "If only we had known, then..."; "If only we had done this, then..."; or "If not for..., then...." Thus the reader becomes involved in the story in as much as a present-day reader can.

In addition, the narrator plays different roles and is assigned various functions in the story. In one such role, the narrator appears wearing the mantle of a historian. Departing from his narrative style – as he frequently does – he employs a summary style with a dramatic flavor by stating, "The verdict has already been pronounced" (p. 19; 8). However, his objective is not only to place himself in the role of a historian-commentator but also and especially to create a sense of irony. It is exemplified in the statement that follows: "yet the Jews of Sighet continued to smile" (p. 19; 8).

As has been pointed out, the narrator resorts to the interrogative voice. At times, he employs rhetorical questions, presented occasionally in parentheses. These questions function as editorial comments, founded on the practical knowledge of experience and hindsight. Their purpose is to augment the depiction of experience and to express a view concerning values or existential themes on the meaning of the Holocaust. Indeed, these rhetorical questions are very important to an understanding of Wiesel's literary art.

An example for the use of a rhetorical question may be found in the story of the first-person narrator, Eliezer, who relates the events leading to the incarceration of the Jews. He tells about the decree to wear yellow badges which identify the bearers as Jewish, quoting his father's comment, "The yellow star? Oh well, what of it? You don't die of it..." (p. 20; 9). Then the first person's rhetorical question follows immediately in parentheses: "(Poor Father! Of what then did you die?)."

The word *Father* is given a capital *F*; his comment about his father's death may then have an ambiguous meaning as it may refer not only to his natural father but also, or rather, to his Father in Heaven. This line of interpretation gains support later in the development of the story when the death of God is depicted as the central theme of the Holocaust experience.

The tone of the question is introduced in several other ways. In one such instance the narrator employs the device of the 'overflowing' or continuous questions. The first-person protagonist, young Eliezer, asks questions in a direct way; then the narrator, as an adult, continues to ask in the same manner and style. The adult-narrator's tone is that of the inquisitive boy but without the quotation marks. Thus, first comes the boy's question: "'When is our turn coming?' I asked my father." Following his father's reply, the narrator continues in the same style of questioning as if repeating the boy's question, but without the quotation marks (which are provided here): "Where were the people being taken to?" And then the editorial narrator continues with the same line of questioning yet with this post-Holocaust knowledge: "Didn't anyone know yet?" And although it may have been a rhetorical question, the narrator, assuming his role as a historian, provides his answer: "No, the secret was well kept" (p. 27; 15). This interlacing of voices creates tension between a narrative of the story and the assessment, between a vanished past and a continuing present. Yet, it also shapes the image of the storyteller himself who is engaged in an enduring tension between his image as a youth going through the experience of the Holocaust and his image as an adult who appraises that experience after its occurrence.

Due to this dichotomy, the representation of the young protagonist at times appears deficient and is occasionally not convincing in its authenticity. In one instance, Eliezer, upon experiencing an atrocity, is voicing his reactions in the form of questions: "I pinched my face. Was I still alive? Was I awake? I could not believe it. How could it be possible for them to burn people, children, and for the world to keep silent? No, none of this could be true" (p. 42; 30). Some of the description and the questions are indeed authentic, yet the reference to the silent world seems to be the projection of the adult narrator.

Moché, the Man of God

Dealing with such an authentic story of a Holocaust experience raises questions concerning any artistic enhancement of the literary composition. In spite of the autobiographical elements of the story, an artist's hand is clearly at work in the structure of the story and the characterization of its protagonists. The prologue establishes the persona of Moché the Beadle as a symbolic figure that sheds its light on the whole work. It may even have its implication over the perception of the Holocaust itself as it gives a literary expression to the essence of the question as an authoritative religious component of the theology of the Holocaust.

Moché's figure was artistically crafted to convey Holocaust-related messages in three spheres of reference. In the sphere of the story's reality, his characterization serves as a premonitory factor, a foreshadowing of what is bound to happen in the story proper to the first-person narrator himself. The Beadle goes through one of the first stages of the Holocaust, being transported by train to the place of extermination. When he returns, miraculously, he informs the people of his experiences and of the atrocities and warns his fellow Jews about what may happen to them, but they do not heed his warnings.

The second sphere adheres to the historical reality. The prologue and Moché's story reflect the naïveté of the Jews in Hungary, as of those in other localities, who did not believe the handwriting on the wall, even when Moché explicitly deciphers the equivalent of the biblical warning "Mene Mene Tekel Upharsin."[5] Several other Holocaust writers, among them Aharon Appelfeld

---

5. See *Daniel* 5:25–28: "Mene – God has numbered [the days of your kingdom and brought it to an end]; Tekel – you have been weighed in the balance

(*Badenheim 1939*, see chapter one), make use of similar ironic material. None of the local Jews believed Moché's stories.

The third sphere of reference is transcendental. Moché appears as a biblical End-of-Days prophet who foretells the end of his fellow Jews. He prophesies not only the future, but also the past (what happened to himself) while alluding to the future. His fate resembles that of the biblical prophets of doom whom no one believed.

Consequently, the critical approach to Wiesel's *Night* evinces that its structure and characterization contribute to the autobiographical story depth and meaning far beyond the personal level of biographical storytelling. Creating this image of Moché the interrogator is imaginatively planned in preparation for the acute existential and theological question that Wiesel is posing.

The Death of God

Unavoidably, the question of faith is a recurring theme in Holocaust literature, especially in literature written by authors who have had a religious upbringing, as is the case of Elie Wiesel. The pre-Holocaust world that Eliezer lived in is depicted in the scene that opens the story: a wholesome Jewish world that is permeated with total faith. It is an all-encompassing traditional way of life as if untouched by modern secularism that affected Jews in communities throughout Europe following the advent of the Haskalah (Jewish Enlightenment), and at its heels, secular Jewish nationalism. This religious milieu may explain the traumatic impact that the ostensibly godless reality of the Holocaust has had on faithful persons. It may further serve as backdrop for the subsequent loss of faith in the reality of the book.

It is of utmost importance to note that the basis for the question discussed so far has already existed among believing Jews whose mouthpiece in the story is Moché the Beadle. Evidently, within the trust-filled boundaries of wholesome faith there is an answer to the question. Indeed, this faithful framework acknowledges that God is omnipotent, and therefore it is man who is inadequate and consequently is incapable of reaching the level of required understanding. Nevertheless, Moché the Beadle's approach prepares the ground by focusing the source of the answer within the human being, within the self (p. 14; 2).

Theological questions have been asked in Jewish writings throughout the ages as Jews were facing terrible persecutions and massacres. Jewish chronicles described those atrocities while implying that they came as punishment from God. Jews have asked, "When will the Messiah come," and

---

[and found wanting]; Peres – your kingdom has been divided [and given to the Medes and the Persians]."

everyday hoped for the coming of the redeemer. While asking, "Where is the Messiah?" Jews have not doubted God and his providence. But the unique experience of the Holocaust gave rise to this troubling question about God.

The reality of the Holocaust came and slapped the believers in God's omnipotence in the face. The survivors of the Holocaust asked, as has the inmate of the concentration camp, "Where is God now? [...] Where is He?" (p. 76; 61). The intensive impact of the Holocaust experience on the faithful Jew is encapsulated in the answer to this question that Eliezer – under the previous guidance of Moché the Beadle – hears within himself as he witnesses the horrid scene of a child's hanging. This brutal act, that has already become emblematic in Holocaust literature, is epitomized by Wiesel as harboring within it that terrible answer to the unfathomable question about God's providence. The given answer: "And I heard a voice within me answer him: 'Where is He? Here He is – He is hanging here on this gallow...'" (p. 76; 62).

Underlying Wiesel's literary representation of the Holocaust experience is the perception of its unique implications to modern civilization and to Judaism. Even to the believer, the implication of the Holocaust with regard to the providence of God is not God's silence, nor his disappearance, but his... death. The cinders of the Holocaust contain the ashes of God, as it were.

However, the death of God concept does not solve the modern Jew's problem of faith. Apparently, Wiesel himself is aware of this, for paradoxically, his theological stance does not deny the existence of God even after the description of his supposed death. Wiesel's autobiographical protagonist is depicted as being troubled by this problem, saying, "Why, but why should I bless Him?" (p. 78; 64). After God's 'death,' Eliezer seems to confront (the dead?) God directly in second-person voice with a question, "What are You, my God?!" (p. 77; 63). Clearly, the personal attachment (use of the possessive case), the direct and close approach of the narrator toward his God does not indicate at all that the problem of the divine has disappeared or that the protagonist manifests a detachment from God, upon the so-called disappearance of God. The relationship between the storyteller and God becomes somewhat more understandable when he establishes the notion of God's betrayal ("...these men here, whom You have betrayed," p. 78; 64), and appoints himself as prosecutor and God as the accused ("I was the accuser, God the accused," p. 79; 65).

A World Without God and Without Man

These accusations do not come easily to one who painted the world of his childhood as a world of all-embracing faith. It appears that God's death is something more than that. It is the death of anything that transcends the individual on the theological as well as on the humanitarian levels; it is the death of mankind, of humanity, in the Holocaust. The reality of the Holocaust has changed not only the narrator's outlook on the world but also the essence of his being and all his links with the world around him. Wiesel, in the words of his first-person protagonist, makes the following remarks about the existential condition of man during the Holocaust (and perhaps also afterwards):

I was alone – terribly alone in a world without God and without man. Without love or mercy. I had ceased to be anything but ashes, yet I felt myself to be stronger than the Almighty, to whom my life had been tied for so long (p. 79; 65).

Eliezer stands as a stranger amidst the inmates that pray to God – his God that had died. This episode ends with an awesome scene of the recitation of the Kaddish, the prayer for the dead, an act so deeply Jewish that it epitomizes the death of all that has been: God, relatives – and man himself. Each individual reciting the Kaddish has died there, though ostensibly he has survived at this point. The incongruous scene of the Jews reciting the Kaddish for themselves, purposely distorts the accepted religious practices: "Everyone recited the Kaddish over his parents, over his children, over his brothers, and over himself" (p. 79; 65). It is intended to represent the Holocaust reality as distorted by blurring the boundaries between life and death. The living may not be distinguishable from those who had been dead.

The reader is expected to conceive the unique reality of *l'univers concentrationnaire* (in David Rousset's terminology)[6] through the distortion of the familiar, day-to-day conventional reality. He is then transferred as an observer to an existential system where death – not life – is the everyday norm. This technique is used by several Holocaust writers, such as Ka-tzetnik and Kosinski, as will be discussed in subsequent chapters.

Despite the recitation of the Kaddish that ironically glorifies and sanctifies the great name of the God who had supposedly died, the notion of God continues to be featured in the theological outlook of the narrator. He is not willing to accept God's silence: "I no longer accepted God's silence" (p. 80; 66), which conveys the message that God exists after his 'death.' Finally, Eliezer rebels against God by eating on Yom Kippur, the Day of Atonement, the most solemn day in the Jewish calendar. He considered it "an act of rebellion and protest against Him" (p. 80; 66), which also expresses his desire to live. This act of defiance reminds one of the other characters in Hebrew literature that have rebelled on Yom Kippur before him (such as Nahman in Feierberg's novel *Whither?*).[7] Yet the protagonist in Wiesel's story has a

---

6. A term based on David Rousset's book by this name, *l'univers concentrationnaire*, published in Paris in 1946, and translated into English as *The Other Kingdom* (New York, 1982), see p. 168. This term is cited and used by Holocaust scholars; see for example, Langer, *The Holocaust and the Literary Imagination*, pp. 15–16, 33.

7. M. Z. Feierburg, *Whither? And Other Stories* (Philadelphia, 1973), p. 126:

unique moral justification for his rebellion that his previous counterparts did not have.

It is evident that Wiesel's *Night* does not profess Jewish atheism. It seems that in Wiesel's theological outlook, which is based on the Holocaust experience, God's existence is not denied. Rather, it maintains that he exists as an entity in negation, in absentia, a modern-day definition of God which somewhat follows the Maimonidian definition of God in the negative. The underlying ontology of the story presents God as a being that does not relate to man – that does not respond to him. The fundamental image in the story of man as the questioner, highlighted as an existential symbol by Moché's words, is represented in light of the Holocaust experience: Man asks, but he does not receive any answer from God who exists as a negative being, an absentee God. God's definition as a negative being, in His non-existent kind of existence, is the answer that man hears bursting forth from the hidden recesses of his soul.

The Agnostic Rabbi

Indeed, loss of faith typifies the Holocaust experience and its major consequence. Loss of faith is exemplified not only by Eliezer in *Night*. Wiesel intensifies the loss of faith as a central motif in the story by depicting a rabbi – the representation of faith and religious authority – who has lost faith in God. He, too, is asking the ultimate religious question of the Holocaust: "Where is God?" and thereby reinforces the very question that has hovered over the scene of the boy's hanging. The rabbi addresses the question by saying, "I can't go on... It's all over," and the narrator explains that "he had no strength left, nor faith" (p. 87; 72). The rabbi's authoritative answer is: "God is no longer with us [...] How can I believe, how could anyone believe, in this merciful God?" (p. 87; 73).

The rabbi deviates from the traditional Jewish answer given during many generations of persecutions and suffering perpetrated against the Jewish people: "For we and our ancestors have sinned" (Prayer on Yom Kippur). The rabbi does not even turn to God in protest as other rabbis and chroniclers have done before him. For example, Yosef ha-Kohen (1496–1575) in his 16th century chronicle: "Will you, oh God, restrain yourself after all this?"[8] The rabbi does not even express his hope for God's salvation and for his revenge as his predecessors have done: "and now I beseech thee, oh God, Lord of the

---

Nahman extinguished a candle on Yom Kippur.

8. Yosef Ha-Kohen, *Emek Habacha* [The Valley of Tears] (Krakau, 1895), Letteris edition, p. 34 [Hebrew].

spirits of all that live! Avenge their vengeance."[9] Nor does he justify God as does Shlomo Ibn Verga (1460–1554): "and God is righteous!"[10]

The Jewish response to past calamities has undergone a major metamorphosis. The rabbi's accusing finger has now turned against heaven.

Another variation, equally touching the heart, of the loss of faith, its result and its meaning, is conveyed through the figure of Akiba Drumer, the believer. The loss of faith causes the believer his own loss, his own demise. Drumer is described as a man whose personal faith has been destroyed and thus causing his own destruction; he loses any desire to persevere in the struggle to exist. His spiritual dying brings about his physical death, echoing in a twisted way the death of Rabbi Akiva, the martyred sage who died in 136 CE (approximately) on Kiddush Hashem (in the Sanctification of the Name, martyrdom).[11]

Which of these two paradigms best fits the character of Eliezer? Perhaps both. Like the rabbi, Eliezer, too, has ceased to believe, as he could no longer believe in God. Like Drumer, Eliezer is left as a living corpse without his faith (p. 126; 109). But unlike these two characters, Eliezer has survived such horrid atrocities which humanity has never witnessed in all its history. According to him, he has survived after God had perished with the millions of others in the Holocaust. As he says upon his struggle about the eclipse of God, "I felt myself to be stronger than the Almighty" (p. 79; 65).

This pronouncement can be seen as Wiesel's intrinsic message of the Holocaust experience and his loss of faith. Man has survived despite God's death, and therefore man is stronger. The author illustrates this message with another description of a conversation with God (who, ostensibly, does not exist), which seems, on the face of it, to contradict the spirit of the story. Eliezer is described as delivering a prayer to God to strengthen him so that he would not act like the son of Rabbi Eliahou who wanted to get rid of his father (p. 104; 87).

This internal and external struggle to sustain the life of his father may be explained as reflecting Eliezer's subconscious and innately imbedded desire to preserve his God. The term "Father," as mentioned above, may refer also to his Father in Heaven ("Poor Father," p. 21; 9). His father has represented the world of Orthodox Judaism. Eliezer's ambivalent attitude to his father's death ("I had no more tears […] free at last!" – p. 124; 106) may illustrate subconsciously his ambiguous position in relation to his loss of faith.

On the conscious level, Eliezer's prayer attests to his struggle to preserve some human value in the face of Holocaust atrocities, perhaps as a substitute

---

9. *Ibid.*
10. Shlomo Ibn Verga, *Shevet Yehudah* [The Sceptre of Judah], The 63rd Persecution, pp. 133–134, Levin Epstein Edition (Jerusalem, n.d.) [Hebrew].
11. See Preface on the ten Jewish martyrs.

for the religious value that had been lost. The reality of the extermination camps prevented any altruism. The existence and survival of the individual seem to stand above any social or moral consideration. The Head of the Block, who speaks as a representative of that reality, advises Eliezer,

Listen to me, boy. Don't forget that you're in a concentration camp. Here, every man has to fight for himself and not think of anyone else. Even of his father. Here, there are no fathers, no brothers, no friends. Everyone lives and dies for himself alone (p. 122; 105).

Yet the value of man, the close contact with fellow men, and the sense of mutual responsibility, were values that were nonetheless preserved within the extermination camps despite the efforts of the oppressors to destroy them. Man's humanity and his spirit survived in the broken bodies and possibly these very qualities kept the bodies alive. Father and son withstood all hardships as they struggled to preserve the dignity of man in conditions created to achieve the very opposite aim. Despite the destruction of the spirit of humanism and of (supposed?) enlightenment in the Holocaust, the fight to maintain the value of man helped man's very chance to survive.[12] Primo Levi refers to similar notions in his book *Survival in Auschwitz,* which is discussed in a later chapter.

Obviously, it will be difficult for anyone who has not experienced the Holocaust to state the above hypothesis with the strength of truth found in Wiesel's book. Wiesel's truth is presented in its impressive simplicity, but with a horrifying frankness. The writer characterizes his protagonist as struggling with himself whether to give a plate of soup to his dying father. And when he does give it, he exposes himself mercilessly to self-criticism lest he has failed the test, as has Rabbi Eliyahou's son (p. 119; 102). The father's death does not bring tears to his eyes, only a feeling of freedom, incomprehensible to an outsider, painful but true, pulsating deeply in his heart: "free at last!" (p. 124; 106).

---

12. See discussion on this topic in Terrence des Pres, *The Survivor* (New York, 1976), Chapter 5.

Chapter 3
Primo Levi: *Survival in Auschwitz* – An Essay on Man

Primo Levi's *Survival in Auschwitz* has achieved a place of prominence in twentieth-century world literature and has become a classic in literature of the Holocaust. Levi's insights, sensitivities, and profound perception make his book a must reading for students of the Holocaust as well as students of literature in general.[1]

It is a literary work which may be summarized by the title "An Essay on Man" if one is to borrow a title from eighteenth-century English poet Alexander Pope. Indeed, the first edition of the English translation was published under the title *If This Is a Man*, which is a more accurate – and a more appropriate – rendering of the title in Italian. Primo Levi's book contains general observations about the condition of man during the Holocaust, timeless comments and timely conclusions, intriguing thoughts, and profound insights.

Primo Levi tells the story of his experience in Auschwitz, but his narrative transcends the story of one man's experience in a concentration camp and becomes an intense and pensive literary record of the destruction of the inmates in body and spirit by Nazi Germany – and the survival of some.

Levi's work was reviewed and assessed by Aharon Appelfeld whose own literary accomplishment was discussed in a previous chapter. Appelfeld stated that long ago Levi's book was taken off the shelf of the testimonial books and was added, without any reservation, to modern literature. "Already in his first book, *If This Is a Man* [which appears in the current edition under the title *Survival in Auschwitz*], it was obvious that we don't have here a person testifying, but a witness who is attempting to examine and to assess his testimony." Appelfeld regards Primo Levi as a

---

1. Primo Levi, *Survival in Auschwitz* (New York, 1996).

Renaissance man [...], a scientist who endeavors to describe in exact details, a humanist who is attached to the Italian and European literature and thought. As a person who was in the inferno for two years, his work is an extensive depiction of suffering, degradation, and shame, but it is also a great wonder about the European culture that made Auschwitz possible. [...] In Auschwitz, European culture disappeared and left behind the demon-man. [...] Primo Levi observed the victims, their low-echelon rigid torturers, who were appointed over the fate of these unfortunate victims. [...] Primo Levi examines, attempts to understand, but he does not judge. [...] The essence of Primo Levi is not abstract ideas, but a detailed description of people and situations. He examines carefully the cutting edge between the dead and the living and excels in his observations.[2]

Primo Levi himself reveals his own intentions in the introduction to *Survival in Auschwitz*. Levi states that his book "has not been written in order to formulate new accusations; it should be able, rather, to furnish documentation for a quiet study of certain aspects of the human mind. [...] The story of the death camps should be understood by everyone as a sinister alarm-signal."[3]

The book should serve as a warning signal for those who consider "every stranger [to be] an enemy." He stresses the need to tell the story "to 'the rest,' to make 'the rest' participate in it [...]. The book has been written to satisfy this need [...] as an interior liberation" (p. 9).

•

"I was captured by the Fascist Militia on 13 December 1943. I was twenty-four, with little wisdom, no experience and a decided tendency [...] to live in an unrealistic world of my own, a world inhabited by civilized Cartesian phantoms, by sincere male and bloodless female friendships" – so does Primo Levi open his story. From the very start one notices the quality of his observations and the unique way he tells his experience.

Retrospective View

Primo Levi enriches his writing by using several literary devices. Rather than just relating an event, Levi is presenting it, at times, with a retrospective view based on knowledge that was learned only after the event and gained during the time of writing. While this literary device is not unique to Primo Levi, for we have seen it in Elie Wiesel's *Night*, his is more sophisticated and

---

2.   Aharon Appelfeld, [Review of Primo Levi's book], *Sfarim* Literary Supplement of *Haaretz* Daily, September 25, 2002 [Hebrew].

3.   Primo Levi, "Author's Preface," *Survival in Auschwitz*, p. 9.

is based not on presenting factual data but on pensive observations and insightful conclusions about life – and death – in the camp.

At the outset, as he is captured by the Italian Militia, the first-person narrator apologizes for not fleeing and forming a partisan band, noting a lesson he learned afterwards as part of the death camp experience: "At that time I had not yet been taught the doctrine I was later to learn so hurriedly in the Lager [the camp]: that man is bound to pursue his own ends by all possible means, while he who errs but once pays dearly" (p. 13). This lesson in regard to any possible action that he could have taken before incarceration comes belatedly to the inmate; however, it did help him survive afterwards.

Typically, such retrospective is made while viewing the past but projecting much later into the 'future' – after the war. Describing the transport in the train, the narrator has the post-Holocaust knowledge that "Among the forty-five people in my wagon only four saw their homes again" (pp. 17–18). Planting this information at this point intensifies the enormity of the tragedy while using the emotive phrase "saw their homes again," as compared to the less effective words "were killed." In some instances the narrator marks the time gap of his post-Holocaust knowledge inserting it into the Holocaust time-frame. He writes: "Today, however [...] we know that of our convoy no more than ninety-six men and twenty-nine women entered the respective camps [...] and that of all the others, more than five hundred in number, not one was living two days later" (p. 20).

Now, this kind of retrospective of viewing the past with the knowledge of the future, and writing the past with such 'foreknowledge,' as it were, creates another dimension of time, which is neither the past nor the future. It allows the reader not only to read about the past, as in any other literary narrative, but also to gain insight into its consequences.

Moreover, it is a very effective way to translate the enormous, unfathomable number of six million murdered into its components, which the human mind can more easily grasp, that of 500 persons not a single one was alive after two days. Learning about the consequences of the Holocaust concurrent with the depiction of events and experiences adds a sense of bitter irony, as the reader knows quite well that the numbers exceed 500.

Sense of Irony Prevails

The sense of irony that abounds in his novel is indeed one of the characteristics of Primo Levi's writings which make reading them an elevating experience. As the definition of irony implies, the writer signals, through some clue, a meaning that runs contrary to the literal denotation of the word, or else creates a sense of contradiction from what is anticipated in order to indicate some detachment or incongruity. Thus, the reader should be aware that he must delve into the text and understand the author's covert intention as diametrically opposite to what he is actually saying.[4]

Tracing the mentality of the inmates in the early stages of their incarceration in the detention camp, the narrator observes with a sense of irony that "A few had given themselves up spontaneously [...] – absurdly – 'to be in conformity with the law'" (p. 14), thus enabling their own imprisonment. This sense of irony reveals insights into the state of mind and naïveté of the internees. A sense of irony prevails as the internees learn "with relief" that they were going to Auschwitz: "We had learnt of our destination with relief. Auschwitz: a name without significance for us at that time, but it at least implied some place on this earth" (p. 17). How could they have known?! And the reader does know at this point what they were about to learn later. The choice of words, stating that at that time they thought that Auschwitz was at least "some place on this earth," harbors within it the irony that afterwards, once they became acquainted with the place, Auschwitz was considered to be another planet (see later chapter on Ka-tzetnik).

Through his unique perception, Primo Levi finds extraordinary situations in this harsh reality. He makes an acute ironic observation: "It was the very discomfort" that they suffered, "the blows, the cold, the thirst that kept us aloft in the void of bottomless despair, both during the journey and after" (p. 17). It is a comment on human spirit and its ability to withstand great difficulties. It may also send a message to the reader about the meaning of the Shoah – one of many offered by Primo Levi: while the Nazis intended to annihilate the Jews both in body and spirit, they definitely failed in the latter goal.

The irony at times turns to be more biting, acerbic, and pungent, and thus it becomes sarcasm.[5] On the senseless murder of little children and the haphazard selection of those destined to be sent to the crematoria (as they climbed down from one side of the convoy rather than the other), the narrator comments: "This is the reason why three-year-old Emilia died: the historical necessity of killing the children of Jews was self-demonstrative to the Germans" (p. 20). When compared to Wiesel's powerful depiction of the hanging of the boy in *Night*, which transcends its meaning on the symbolic level (see the chapter on Elie Wiesel's *Night*), Primo Levi's depiction is sarcastic, but is more specific and includes details about this child. She was not just an anonymous girl; he provides her name and her father's, and he goes on to tell about her personality. She was the daughter

---

4.   On the term and its definition, see D. C. Meucke, *The Compass of Irony* (London, n.d.), chap. 2.

5.   For additional definitions, see *ibid.*, p. 54; Gilbert Highet, *The Anatomy of Satire* (Princeton, 1962), p. 57.

of Aldo Levi of Milan, and "was curious, ambitious, cheerful, intelligent child" (p. 20). While she serves as a representation of the murdered children of the Holocaust, she is a real person. The use of the tone of irony or sarcasm makes her loss emotionally touching, and the senseless futility of her murder cries out.

Landscape Depiction

Some Holocaust writers pay special attention to describe the landscape surrounding the sites of the death camps. Some do it in order to enhance the realism as background to the atrocities, or conversely to highlight its symbolic implication. Primo Levi depicts the landscape associated with the inmates' experiences in the death camps in a way that presents his unique view and profound perception epitomizing this particular situation. Most appropriately, the author's portrayal of the landscape is presented as though seen through the inmates' eyes, thus making it more authentic and more devastating. He describes sunrise: "Dawn came on us like a betrayer; it seemed as though the new sun rose as an ally of our enemies to assist in our destruction" (p. 16). He tells the reader that the sun sets "in a tumult of fierce, blood-red clouds" (p. 29). He describes these clouds elsewhere as "malevolent clouds" (p. 42). Similar attributes of the sun are found, for example, in Ka-tzetnik's writings, but they are used more as static symbols, which by themselves are quite powerful. Levi's imagery is more succinct, tied directly to the scene, and reflects the perception of the inmates. To them, "Around us, everything is hostile" (p. 42).

Portrayal of Inmates

Equally impressive is Primo Levi's portrayal of inmates. It is presented from the perspective of a fellow inmate, but it is a view of a by-stander from some needed distance, which paradoxically allows the narrator to come close to the inmates and also bring them closer to the reader. The portrayal of people is picturesque and done not without a touch of humor. Their walking, for example, seems to be peculiar: "They walked [...] with an odd, embarrassed step, head dangling in front, arms rigid. On their heads they wore comic berets and were all dressed in long striped overcoats, which even by night and from a distance looked filthy and in rags" (p. 20). This first encounter of the newcomers with veteran inmates may have its humorous touch. But the harsh realization comes crashing on them: "We looked at each other without a word. It was incomprehensible and mad, but one thing we had understood. This was the metamorphosis that awaited us. Tomorrow we would be like them" (pp. 20–21).

What seems to be a portrayal of an external look turns out to be an insight into the inmates' own perceptions of themselves upon the bitter realization that they, too, will be and will look like, the veteran internees. And indeed, they later assume the same look and the same identity. Primo Levi's descriptions reveal their hidden thoughts and feelings authentically: "...we do not dare lift our eyes to look at one another. There is nowhere to look in a mirror, but our appearance stands in front of us, reflected in a hundred livid faces, in a hundred miserable and sordid puppets. We are transformed into the phantoms glimpsed yesterday evening" (p. 26).[6]

As the transformation has been completed, Levi later portrays the new internees as walking "with a strange, unnatural hard gait, like stiff puppets made of jointless bones" (p. 30), a phantasmagoria of human shadows, scarecrows who scare themselves.

Unlike in some of the other Holocaust writings, Primo Levi portrays his fellow inmates with vivid and colorful detail, and thus the reader is exposed to a variety of people from all walks of life and from different backgrounds and countries. Thus he tells of "small Wachsmann" who was a rabbi, "in fact a Melamed, a person learned in the Torah," who was known in his village in Galicia to be a healer. Levi marveled at the amazing vitality of this man working for two years without falling ill and for spending long evenings discussing Talmudic matters in Yiddish and Hebrew with Mendi, who was a modernist rabbi (p. 68).

A colorful inmate was Elias, a dwarf, who became an excellent worker, and an epitome of surviving in the camp. Pondering about Elias, Levi surmises that he endured all the camp's atrocities "because he was physically indestructible; he has resisted the annihilation from within because he is insane." Levi's conclusion is that Elias survived because "he is the most adaptable, the human type most suited to this way of living" (p. 97). This tongue-in-cheek assessment summarizes Primo Levi's view of *l'univers concentrationnire* in its madness. Through this characterization, Levi was able to enliven an enigmatic inmate in a meaningful way and to comment on the nature of survival in Auschwitz.

The inmate Henri, on the other hand, was different. He was civilized and sane, and he devised three methods to escape extermination while still able to "retain the name of man: organization [traffic in products], pity and theft" (p. 98). Levi concludes his discussion of Henri with the post-Holocaust knowledge that Henri is alive at the time of writing, and that he – Levi – would want to know "his life as a free man"; but the loaded punch line is that he would not want to see Henri again (p. 100).

---

6.   "Puppets" – in the translation into the Hebrew version of the book it translates to "scarecrow." Elsewhere they are described as "mud puppets" (p. 133).

Among others, there is a devastating portrayal of "Null Achtzehn" (Zero Eighteen), who apparently has forgotten his name. He is a number. At this point "he gives the impression of being empty inside [...] like the slough of certain insects which one finds on the banks of swamps" (p. 42). All in all, at the end Levi admits that the personages depicted in his book "are not men. Their humanity is buried, or they themselves have buried it, under an offence received or inflicted on someone else" from the "evil and insane SS men, the Kapos" to the "slave Häftlinge [prisoners]" (pp. 121–122). Excluded from the group of victims and victimizers was an Italian civilian worker, Lorenzo, who gave him a piece of bread and remnants of his ration for six months, and also gave him his vest. Lorenzo wrote a postcard on his behalf to Italy and brought him back a reply, for which he did not ask for anything nor would he accept any reward. He did it "because he was good and simple and did not think that one did good for a reward" (p. 119).

The author believes that he is alive today because of Lorenzo; not so much because of the material things he gave him, but because Lorenzo's goodness reminded him that behind the barbed wires there still existed a just world, or at least "a remote possibility of good" for which "it was worth surviving" (p. 121). Compared to the others cited above, "Lorenzo was a man," Primo Levi declares; "his humanity was pure and uncontaminated, he was outside this world of negation." And he states, "Thanks to Lorenzo, I managed not to forget that I myself was a man" (p. 122).

Levi's depiction of inmates is full of insights into human nature which allows the reader to gain a glimpse into the lives and the experiences of these people.

Observations of the Inmates' State of Mind

It is the quality of description with profound assessment of people and conditions and acute observations that typify Primo Levi's writing. He is indeed an observer par excellence. He describes scenes and inmates' feelings in detail with all their complexities. It is noticeable when he deals with people's reaction to their incarceration, upon the transition from supposedly free people to internees: "The different emotions that overcame us, of resignation, of futile rebellion, of religious abandon, of fear, of despair, now joined together after a sleepless night in a collective, uncontrolled panic" (p. 16). It is a summary in detail, showing a span of human emotions and attitudes felt by the group.

At times, the narrator would come up with a simple statement about the inmates that purposefully avoids giving information but is so true and authentic in what it does not say. For example, at the incarceration Levi reports, "Many things were then said and done among us; but of these it is better that there remain no memory" (p. 16). In a similar vein, he would comment on the Italian inmates who first met every Sunday and then ceased because it was too sad to see fewer and fewer people coming each time: "It was so tiring to walk those few steps and then, meeting each other, to remember and to think. It was better not to think" (p. 37). It is the honest reflection of their state of mind facing the cruel reality of the extermination.

His observations and reflections on human nature as the inmates react to some minor atrocities may surprise the reader with his original insight: the first blows they received were "so new and senseless that we felt no pain, neither in body nor in spirit." The result was "Only a profound amazement: how can one hit a man without anger?" (p. 16).

Pensive Generalization, Reflections, Thoughts

Some of the author's reflections about the circumstances and conditions of the camp and its inmates appear in the form of general observations about man and his predilections. At times they may constitute concise statements based on life experience, insights into human drives that sound like aphorisms. For example, at an early stage of his capture, Levi cites the doctrine which was mentioned earlier in the chapter that he was to learn later in camp: that "man is bound to pursue his own ends by all possible means, while he who errs but once pays dearly" (p. 13), which turns out to be a motto for survival.

Upon incarceration, the narrator makes a general observation about the nature of living under such destructive conditions. "Sooner or later in life everyone discovers that perfect happiness is unrealizable, but there are few who pause to consider the antithesis: that perfect unhappiness is equally unattainable" (p. 17). It is here that the aphorism is appealing not only because of its crisp, catchy structure, but because of the insightful message about the Job-like sufferings of the inmates, which is providing an ironic hint of consolation.

In the kingdom of death the author reaches a devastating but honest conclusion that "There are few men who know how to go to their deaths with dignity, and often they are not those whom one would expect" (p. 18). And on suffering, he opines, "human nature is such that grief and pain – even simultaneously suffered – do not add up as a whole in our consciousness, but hide, the lesser behind the greater" (p. 73).

These overall observations and pensive comments create general concepts of epitaph quality that attribute an existential expression to the Holocaust experience, transcending the experience itself. They are indicative of the exceptional quality of Primo Levi's writing.

Historical Perspective and Literary Allusions

In addition to his reflections on the human condition, Primo Levi endows his writing with a 'depth of vision' which relates the Holocaust experience to Jewish and world literature. It enriches the reading of his novel as a literary experience, adding contextual references to external literature and thus contributing to the understanding of his theme. In preparation for the transport, the Jews conduct themselves as if in mourning, placing Yahrzeit (Memorial) candles, praying and weeping, as the narrator expresses the emotions of the inmates in light of past tragedies in Jewish history: "and we experienced within ourselves a grief that was new for us, the ancient grief of the people that has no land, the grief without hope of the exodus which is renewed every century" (p. 16). While they are modern Jews who have not experienced any expulsion or pogrom before, they now can relate to similar events in Jewish history while having no hope for a miraculous exodus.

The stories that the inmates tell each other of sufferings and cruelties that had happened to them are described by the narrator as "simple and incomprehensible like the stories in the Bible," and then he adds the punch line, "But are they not themselves stories of a new Bible?" (p. 66). These are stories of doom and gloom that will add another book of sorrow to the Jewish scriptures. The tower which they built near the factory where they worked and the many nationalities therein remind the author of the Tower of Babel, as indeed it is called by them. Its bricks "were cemented by hate; hate and discord" like its biblical namesake. To the inmates, a curse hangs over the "insolent building based on the confusion of languages and erected in defiance of heaven" (p. 73). The biblical story of the Tower of Babel serves as a subtext for the modern-day edifice built to express "our masters [...] contempt for God and men" (p. 73).

From world literature Levi enlists most appropriately Dante's *Inferno* to relate to his experience as he cites from Dante's *Divine Comedy* (p. 112), and relates its depiction of hell to the camps: "This is hell. Today, in our times, hell must be like this" (p. 22). From Greek literature he mentions the Tantalus myth in reference to suffering (pp. 61–62). A German soldier who asked his prisoners for money or wallets which will be of no use to them is referred to as a modern-day Charon who, in Greek mythology, is in charge of transferring the souls of the dead across the river Styx and deprives them of their worldly possessions (p. 21).

These allusions to world literature enrich Levi's novel with subtexual references which add meaning to his story and relates it to the classical literary tradition. They prove that the spirit of humanism was kept alive and perhaps sustained the inmates despite the conditions that intended to destroy it. They also pose the great humanist tradition of Western civilization versus its antithesis in Nazi ideology.

Camp's Reality, Rules and Morality

The transferring of the prisoners from freedom to confinement over the proverbial river Styx happens upon their initiation into the reality of the death camps. Primo Levi presents this transition with cruel details: they are being numbered with a tattoo, and then they are introduced to "a new order" of the concentration camp that "took place in a grotesque and sarcastic manner" (p. 28). Its rules are different than what they were familiar with; they are told that "in this place everything is forbidden" (p. 29). Following a detailed physical depiction of the camp (pp. 31–32), the rules that govern it are presented as a codex from another planet: "the normal order of things" is "that the privileged oppress the unprivileged." This is the social structure of the camp which is based on this human law (p. 44).

Under these laws and social structure, the question of morality, such as theft, does not pose any major problem, although the rules are confusing and contradictory: theft in the Buna (the work factory) is authorized and encouraged by the SS; theft in the camps, repressed by the SS, is considered by the civilians as "a normal exchange operation"; and theft among the inmates is punishable, and both the thief and the victim are equally punished. Against this confusing system of justice, the narrator invites the reader to evaluate the meaning of such words as 'good' and 'evil' or 'just' and 'unjust' in the context of the camp, and judge "how much of our ordinary moral world could survive on this side of the barbed wire" (p. 86).

Very few could survive, he concludes, without renouncing some part of their moral world (p. 92), and, as discussed before, Levi shows how some of the inmates managed to survive despite all odds.

The Inmates' Goal: Survive to Bear Witness

As seen in other writings, inmates' incentives to survive assume various expressions. Some writers express their wish to survive in order to bear witness, while others explained their wish to go on living in order to disprove the very intention of the Nazis to destroy the Jews. Indeed, Primo Levi reflects on this goal and attempts to show the way to survive in spite of all hardships and adverse conditions. He argues that even in this place one can survive, "and therefore one must want to survive, to tell the story, to bear witness." In order to survive, one must force himself to retain at least "the skeleton, the scaffolding, the form of civilization" (p. 41). This is Levi's declaration of humanism: in spite of their enslavement, deprivation of every right, exposure to insult, and condemnation to death, the inmates still possess "the power to refuse our consent"; and it should be defended at all costs. Thus, they should wash their faces without soap in dirty water, and dry themselves on their clothes and polish their shoes – not because of the regulations but "for dignity and propriety." Also, they should go erect without dragging their feet in order "to remain alive, not to begin to die" (p. 41). It is a very powerful message in its simplicity and authenticity that the survivor can relay to his reader.

And Levi has also a message to humanity as if from inside the Lager (the camp) for free men outside: "take care not to suffer in your own homes what is inflicted on us here" (p. 55).

Concurrent with the message to humanity, Primo Levi attempts to explain the inmates' condition, knowing that it would be difficult for an outsider to understand it in full. Primo Levi starts with the mundane, the deprivation of all prior habits and possessions, let alone comforts – matters which the reader can easily understand. It is here, as in other similar instances, that the author finds it necessary to speak directly to the reader: "Imagine now a man who is deprived of everyone he loves, and at the same time of his house, his habits, his clothes, in short of everything he possesses: he will be a hollow man, reduced to suffering and needs, forgetful of dignity and restraint, for he who loses all often easily loses himself" (p. 27).

Inquisitive and analytical, Primo Levi tenaciously pursues his natural inclination to understand what is happening and to try to explain it to the reader. He attempts to understand the acts of 'initiation' into the camp as their civilian clothes were taken and they were shaven and sheared, and then taken naked to the cold shower. He concludes that all of this is done in order to degrade and humiliate them ("all this is a game to mock and sneer at us," p. 24), although he is fully aware that the ultimate goal is to kill them. Of course, the final solution was no game, as the inmates were to learn later.

Levi undertook to explain and analyze some daily activities; for example, the marching from the camp to work and back with the music playing marches and popular songs. From some distance ("even today"), Primo Levi remembers "those innocent songs" and his blood freezes in his vein. The tunes "lie engraven on our minds and will be the last thing in Lager that we shall forget." They are "the voice of the Lager," exhibiting "the resolution of others to annihilate us first as men in order to kill us more slowly afterwards." The music in this "monstrous rite" causes them to march like "automatons; their souls are dead and the music drives them, like the wind drives dead leaves, and takes the place of their will". The SS watch them march like this, seeing in them "concrete proof of their victory" (p. 51).

The very inquiry, engaging in analysis and reflection, as exemplified by Primo Levi in the above depictions, kept the human spirit alive despite the Nazis' attempts to annihilate them body and soul.

Style, Literary Devices and Techniques

Primo Levi's style of writing is very intense as he presents the day-to-day life in the camp. He writes in the present tense ("A band begins to play," p. 30;

"Alberto is my best friend," p. 57; "Today is working Sunday," p. 126), which enables the reader to feel a sense of presence, immediacy, and close proximity. As will be discussed in a following chapter, it is a technique used by Katzetnik for similar purposes.

Use of metaphors abounds in his writing and Levi uses them selectively to reflect the conditions in the camp. Thus, the steam-shovel is described as opening its mouth and snapping the soil "voraciously," as the inmates, suffering their gnawing hunger, cannot turn away their eyes from looking at "the steam-shovel's meal" (p. 74). The sights of the early stages of incarceration seem to them as if they were "watching some mad play," with "witches, the Holy Spirit and the devil" (p. 25), a reference, perhaps, to medieval morality plays.

Various figures of speech are also used. Personification is one such device. The narrator reports that "Massacre moves through the huts [...] every day" (p. 53), which makes the atrocity a real entity in the death camps. Levi refers to Auschwitz using different loaded terms such as, "the house of the dead" (p. 31); the life of the "Ka-Be [the hospital] is a life of limbo" (p. 50), that transitory place bordering hell or heaven.

Levi's attitude toward language is of interest. He is aware of the weakness of language to express the unfathomable experience of the Holocaust in full. As they move into the realm of the "other planet," Levi records their reaction, saying, "for the first time we became aware that our language lacks words to express this offence" (p. 26).

There is a fascinating description of the German officer commanding the inmates through an interpreter to be quiet and not make noise: "You must be quiet, because this is not a rabbinical school." Levi observes that "the words which are not his, the bad words, twist his mouth as they come out, as if he was spitting out a foul taste" (p. 24). Language seems to be more than just a means of communication.

Language in the concentration camp functions differently than in the outside world. Similarly, words expressing certain needs or conditions have different meaning in the current reality; for example, "hunger is not that feeling of missing a meal," so is "cold" for which there is a need for a new word. "We say 'hunger', we say 'tiredness', 'fear', 'pain', we say 'winter' and they are different things. They are free words, created and used by free men who live in comfort and suffering in their homes" (p. 123). Dictionary words with which we are familiar with have had different denotations, let alone connotations, in the camps.

While attesting to the weakness of language to express the experience of the death camps, Primo Levi is able through his own mastery of language to express just that, as a keen observer and a brilliant, sensitive, and authentic artist.

Chapter 4
Ka-tzetnik: 'Star of Ashes' Becomes *Star Eternal* – Depiction of Another Planet

One of the authors who devoted his writings almost totally to the Holocaust is a survivor – the Hebrew and Yiddish writer, Yehiel Dinur, better known as Ka-tzetnik.[1] Under the pen name of Ka-tzetnik, Dinur has published widely on the experiences of the Holocaust, and many of his works have been translated into English and are available to the English reader. In his literary work and his public image, Dinur was considered one of the major spokesmen of the survivors.

Yehiel Dinur may be remembered from his testimony at the Eichmann trial in Jerusalem in 1961, on which occasion he fainted as he was overcome by his emotions and memories. Undoubtedly, both his emotions and memories are the foundation of his work. Yet, his own definition of his literary endeavor may shed light on his perception of his own work. He said,

> I do not consider myself as an author writing literature. It is chronicles [that I write] out of the planet Auschwitz. I was there approximately two years. But time there is not the same as it is here on earth; every split second there moves on different cogs of time. The inhabitants of that planet did not have names. They did not have parents, nor did they have children. They did not dress the way people dress here; they were not born, and did not give birth; they breathed in accordance with some other rules of nature. They did not live by the laws of this world here, nor did they die [by them]. Their name was the number Ka-tzetnik.[2]

Some critics accepted his statement that he was not writing literature at face value. In 1972, an Israeli reviewer cited his early encounter with

---

1. 'Ka-tzet' is the pronunciation of K.Z., the abbreviation of Konzentration Zentrum – concentration camp. The inmate was known as Ka-tzetnik.
2. Shammai Golan, ed., *Hashoah, Pirkei Edut Vesifrut* [The Holocaust: Eye-Witness and Literary Accounts] (Tel Aviv, 1976), p. 177 [Hebrew].

Ka-tzetnik's writings as a teenager and his shock of learning about the Holocaust. Yet, a few years later, that reviewer approached Ka-tzetnik's books more critically and concluded that "Ka-tzetnik's books are not literature. Not in characterization, nor in the organization of plot. Not in outlook or in language which lacks minimal quality." This critic suggested that the Holocaust, "that cardinal event which tore the annals of humanity into two – before and after – cannot be expressed with literary tools." As for Ka-tzetnik, the reviewer believes that he fell between the two chairs – between literature and chronicles."[3]

If Ka-tzetnik is not writing 'literature,' what is it that he wrote? Is it a work of 'fiction'? Definitely not in the sense that writers such as Bartov, Gouri, and Amichai, who will be discussed later, wrote fiction. So, can his writings be considered chronicles, as he has asserted? No; not in the sense of a documentary, handling names, documents, facts. Neither does it have the format of a diary or memoirs.

Of course, to address the question "Does he write literature?" we need to define 'literature.' If we define it for the sake of brevity as "imaginative expression of human experience," it is possible to answer the question in the affirmative. Yet if we look for the literary tools or the literary treatment found in the modern novel, we will have difficulties finding them in Ka-tzetnik's writing.

It seems that we have to approach Ka-tzetnik's writings as a unique literature, literature of atrocity, that may have its own literary criteria, as discussed in previous chapters, while still weighing in the background criteria of 'conventional' literature. We should examine his work on its own merit, reconstructing Ka-tzetnik's literary criteria as found in this work.

To this end, this chapter will examine one of Ka-tzetnik's most impressive works, a small book, which has the English title *Star Eternal*. It was originally published in Hebrew in 1960, and the English translation appeared in 1971.[4]

Star Eternal is a story of the Holocaust experience in Auschwitz, with a prologue and an epilogue both having the same locale, the narrator's city of Metropoli. The book ends with an editorial statement of great emotional impact concerning reparation, which, regardless of significance, seems to have been artificially attached to the book.

The Before and After Effect

---

3. H. B., "K. Tzetnik," *Keshet*, XV (No. 1, Fall 1972), pp. 188–189 [Hebrew]. A more favorable review by another Israeli critic, Mordechai Ovadyahu, appears in *Besa'ar Uvidemamah* [In Storm and Silence] (Tel Aviv, 1976), pp. 82–90 [Hebrew].

4. Ka-tzetnik, *Kochav Ha'efer* [Star of Ash] (Israel, 1966) [Hebrew]; Ka-tzetnik 135633, *Star Eternal* (New York, 1971).

The structure of the story as such, having a prologue and an epilogue, is intended to achieve the "before and after" effect – that is, before and after the Holocaust. The story unfolds in the autumn of 1939, a few days before the war, and ends immediately after the war. In between the two dates, the narrator relates his experience at the "other planet," Auschwitz. He uses many parallels in the prologue and the epilogue, such as the clock, the Hall of Justice, and the statue of the Goddess of Justice (pp. 11, 13). Indeed, these parallels become significant symbols, which epitomize the Holocaust experience.

The clock showing the same time before and after the Holocaust evokes the notion that time stood still during the Holocaust, that history 'stopped,' as it were, from its flow for this unparalleled event. Thus, one may deduce that the Holocaust was unique in the history of mankind. Yet on the other hand it may also imply that nothing had really changed since the Holocaust and that the clock continued to tick from the time it stopped for the duration of the war. Another very powerful message is that justice is blind, like its symbol the blindfolded Goddess of Justice. Similarly, the sun's light that appears to shine before and after the war strengthens this message. The similarity, indeed the parallel, carries a devastating message to the reader: He who returns from the other planet, Auschwitz, realizes, much to his horror, that "Here, nothing has changed" (p. 119). It is the most agonizing conclusion that the author shares with the reader at the end of his depiction of the Holocaust reality, that nothing has changed after Auschwitz. The Hall of Justice has not changed; the Goddess of Justice is still blindfolded – an obvious ironic allusion to the miscarriage of justice, and the hands of the clock continue to show the same time as before, as if nothing has happened from 1939 to 1945.

Although these symbols are not presented in a high degree of literary sophistication or subtlety, their impact on the reader is believed to be significant. One concludes that Ka-tzetnik is at his best when he does not editorialize on aspects of the Holocaust as in the subject of reparations. He is most effective when he lets the reader experience the "before and after" effect and then reach his own conclusion.

The Night of Auschwitz

The structure of the book is based on scenes, more often than not loosely connected to one another: forced labor, transport of the old and the young, and the last transport to Auschwitz. Subsequently, there are a number of chapters devoted to the actual experience of the Holocaust in Auschwitz. These chapters follow a rough course of a day, beginning most appropriately at night – the night of Auschwitz – and ending at the evening roll call. They concentrate on such scenes as entering Auschwitz, the bath house, block curfew, cruelties, prayers, and food. This experience ends in the last parade to the crematorium, at which occasion the theological questions pertaining to the attitude of God toward his people are raised. The chapter ends on a note of hope about some continuity in the land of Israel. Liberation is thereafter thrust upon the narrator and the reader as an act of *deus ex machina*, an unexpected salvation.

Upon reading *Star Eternal*, one should endeavor to look for Ka-tzetnik's unique way of depicting the Holocaust reality as experienced by him. The quality of his style is not the kind which would attract a sophisticated reader for it is rather austere, containing little imagery. Nevertheless, it is this very language – brief, laconic, almost impoverished – that is most appropriate for Ka-tzetnik's subject matter. His language lends itself to abrupt changes, jerks and twists, resembling epileptic seizures. It is as though the author was struggling with words and their ability to translate the reality of atrocity into the medium of verbal expression. His struggle is discerned in the abundance of exclamation points, generally considered a weak device in literature. The statement, "Words are no more" (p. 41), uttered in the context of Auschwitz, typifies the author's perception of language after Auschwitz. This attitude toward language appears to be in concert with George Steiner's view, which was cited in the introduction: "The world of Auschwitz lies outside speech as it lies outside reason."[5] Aware of the limitation of language, the author resorts to the bare linguistic minimum. For example:

"Earth.
"Fifteen men dig one pit in the earth. [...]
"They dig" (p. 17).

Typically, the curt structure of the individual sentences projects to a similar pattern established in the paragraphs and the chapters which are succinct and terse. There are very little descriptions, and where they are found they function as symbols or intend to convey emotions. His use of words is measured as he is very frugal with them. As depicted by Ka-tzetnik through the whole structure of the book, the Holocaust experience is perceived as structurally fragmented; events and time do not flow, they just occur without any logical sequence or order whatsoever.

Thus, there is an artistic attempt to present reality as distorted, as lacking its normal components of time and space. There is no movement in time, in the normal sense, as there is no development of character, essential to any novel. The reader is thus made to experience suspended time and space of the Holocaust reality.

---

5.   George Steiner, *Language and Silence* (New York, 1967), p. 123.

Second-Person Narrative – You

In spite of the apparent austerity in style, Ka-tzetnik does employ a variety of literary devices intended to enhance his message. The most effective of these devices is the second-person narrative pervading most of the book. The opening line of the story reads: "Behind you, in the spacious show-windows..." (p. 11).

Through the employment of the second-person voice – *you!* – Ka-tzetnik attempts in a most effective way to relate the experience of the Holocaust *directly* to the reader. The direct and constant reference to "You!" does have a cumulative effect upon the reader. It makes him not only a direct witness to the experience, but indeed it forces him to experience the reality of the Holocaust in as much as it is possible for a reader. The reader is unable to stay totally detached from this experience as he reads about "You" – being himself! He must become involved. He is there in Auschwitz, in a manner of speaking, together with the narrator.

At times, the reader is made to witness the atrocities as they occur: "The cane rises: Everybody watch now – magic! Nothing up my sleeve! Take a good look! Here before you is a life. Right? In the twinkling of an eye you'll see –"; "See for yourselves" (p. 68). "Here in front of you lies a life" (p. 69).

Furthermore, the reader becomes a victim in the experience of the Holocaust. In one scene, when the Jews are being ordered to dig their own graves, the ubiquitous 'you' is used: "With every thrust of your spade – you bury the sun in the earth [...]. Opposite, reflected in the pupils of your eyes: boots" (p. 17).

The narrator takes the reader to the showers in Auschwitz: "A network of pipes above your head [...]. It's getting packed. Bodies, nude and clammy, around you" (p. 42), and you, a modern reader familiar with the fake showers that emitted deadly gas, can only shudder....

This technique compels the reader to emerge from the normal role as a passive outsider and to relate to the events described, thus getting close to becoming a temporary insider. To use Langer's terminology in *The Holocaust and the Literary Imagination*, "The reader is temporarily an insider and permanently an outsider."[6]

This concept of the reader *being there* tends to shatter the reader's sense of security and his ostensible awareness that it is definitely a story told of past events. Thus, the employment of second-person voice places the reader in that very same predicament as though the literary convention of storytelling no

---

6. Lawrence L. Langer, *The Holocaust and the Literary Imagination* (New Haven, 1975), p. 3.

longer shields him, or at least in the frame of mind that in effect leads him to conclude: "*You could have been there.*" And it is extremely frightening.[7]

Furthermore, by employing the pronoun "you" the author establishes, in a clever way, an unusual rapport between the speaker-narrator and the addressed person, who turns out to be an 'Everyman' figure. Thus, the narrative achieves a point which extends beyond the mere telling of a story. For it is in effect a loaded message, a call for humanity at large to experience the Holocaust and thus for every one to become a survivor.

Continuous Present Tense

Related to this technique is another which employs the present tense in the narrative of the story. Events are described in the book under the illusion of a continuous present tense. As a result, scenes seem to occur in the reader's presence, right *now* and *here*. Combined with the second-person narrative, this technique intensifies the literary reality of the Holocaust as it compels the reader to experience the Holocaust in a literary way. The reality of the Holocaust is thus brought closer to home, while the reader experiences the possibility of his own person going through the catastrophe of the Shoah as a temporary insider, and as a result may consider himself permanently a survivor.

Significantly, the present tense stops abruptly at a major turning point in the story and the narrative is suddenly presented in past tense. It occurs as the end draws near and the inmates are thrown into isolation blocks to await their final transport to the crematorium. It is as though life stopped for these inmates as well as for the reader. They are deemed dead while still being alive; they are already in the realm of the past tense. The narrator explains this ironic phenomenon as follows: "Here there's no longer anyone to fear. Here you're already free of the rules that govern the normal blocks of Auschwitz" (p. 103). Death seems to bring an end to the reality of the Holocaust.

It is at this point that the narrator allows himself a dialogue, omitted almost completely from the total text. The intentional omission of dialogue in order to depict an uncivilized state of humanity is a device used also in Kosinski's book *The Painted Bird*,[8] as discussed in the following chapter. The dialogue in *Star Eternal* centers on the theological questions of the Holocaust and presents a note of hope for the doomed inmates and for Judaism. It is hoped – the dialogue stresses – that elsewhere, namely in the land of Israel, life

---

7.   Compare, for example, Steiner's statement, "I am a kind of survivor," in *Language and Silence*, p. 145, originally published in *Commentary*, Vol. 39 (No. 2, February 1965), p. 32.

8.   See Jerzy Kosinski, *The Painted Bird* (Boston, 1972), and his *Notes of the Author on The Painted Bird* (New York, 1967), p. 16. *Cf.* Langer, *The Holocaust and the Literary Imagination*, p. 168. See chapter 5 on Kosinski below.

goes on – life should go on in spite of the horrendous attempt to eradicate Jews and Jewish life in Europe (p. 108).

It should be remarked that while one does understand the necessity for such a 'transcendental' reasoning about the meaning of the Shoah, it looks somewhat artificial in the way it is presented by the narrator. Ostensibly, it is a post-Holocaust concept that justifies the existence of Israel as a haven for Jews who might face future threats of annihilation. While one is hesitant to set standards on what is authentic and what is not in the context of a literary work on the Jewish catastrophe, one is indeed permitted to get the cues from the author himself elsewhere in the story. Based on comparison, it may be concluded that this rationalization about the Holocaust – namely, that life should go on elsewhere, as presented by Ka-tzetnik – is less effective than other segments of the book which depict the actual experience of the Holocaust. A more subtle way of introducing this notion – which is by itself significant – would have been much more convincing. It should be mentioned that what appears to be an accepted historical theory (that is, the close connection between the Holocaust and the establishment of the State of Israel) – formulated after the Holocaust – may, in the context of relating an authentic Holocaust experience, look like an anachronistically 'planted' rationalization. It is noted in the following dialogue:

"'Rabbi of Shilev,'" Ferber asks, "'for whose sake does Jacob wrestle with the Angel, if his children did not cross the river, but stayed here in the blackness of the night?'"

The Rabbi answers:

"'From the very blackness of this night Jacob will bring forth the name 'Israel.' Before that, the morning star will not rise.'

"Light of full understanding flashed within Ferber: his brothers, there, in the Land of Israel! Revelation bared itself to him. For a split second only" (p. 108).

Nevertheless, this chapter, titled "The Last Argument," is not without its message and significance. It is for the first time that some of the Jewish inmates are identified by name. Previously, a total dehumanization and lack of identity prevailed in the book, a technique which is intended to present a mimetic aspect of concentration camp existence. As the rest of the people are demanding "The ration!!!" (p. 104), Ferber the faithful is engaged in matters which transcend the immediate time and place. He discusses the meaning of the death and suffering with the Rabbi. While drawing heavily on the biblical paradigm of Jacob's struggle with the angel, it should be noted that the outcome of this encounter and its accompanying revelation are no longer perceived in the domain of the divine. The emergence of Israel is totally engulfed by the secular – namely, it is the national continuity of the people in the Land of Israel (p. 108). It looks as though it is divorced from divine providence. Importantly, the religious authority of the Jewish people, the

Rabbi, is made to become the carrier of this secular revelation of the Shoah experience.

God Abandoned This Earth

Upon liberation, the Ka-tzet, the concentration camp inmate, arrives at his own conclusion on the whereabouts of the divine: "God abandoned this earth; Devil, too, turned his back on it" (p. 110). It is not the death of God concept which is promulgated here by Ka-tzetnik.[9] Rather, it is an idea of abandonment by all supernatural powers. Even the Devil, supreme representation of evil, would not have any part in the atrocities of the Shoah.

In spite of the secular and somewhat realistic setting of the chapter "The Last Argument," the author resorts to a mystical and an enigmatic ending as a catharsis. As the end draws near, Ferber feels redeemed: "Roundabout him all was distillate, pure. No longer did he feel himself in his own skeleton. At that moment he was utterly oblivious of his body's existence. The Rabbi's eyes were like two open gates–[.] He entered in unto them" (p. 108). Death is delineated as having not only the power of personal salvation, but as possessing some inexplicable mystical powers of uniting the individual with his national and historical past. Indeed, it is a very subtle way of attempting to give some meaning to the meaningless, illogical, and savage annihilation of the Jews by the Nazis. It brings to bear the historical dimension of the Holocaust, relating this calamity to the tragic fate of the Jewish people throughout its bloody history.

Some of Ka-tzetnik's other techniques are very effective as well. In an attempt to recreate the reality of the Holocaust for the reader, the narrator at times abolishes the borderline between the real and the unreal, between the physical and the metaphysical. He directs a question to 'Life' as if it were an entity that could be addressed: "Life! Life! Who are you?" (p. 69). More overwhelming, perhaps, is the personification of death as an entity, as a concrete essence in the Holocaust experience.

Death is so ingrained in reality that it characterizes the act of living more than life itself does. In this distorted reality, as conceptualized by Ka-tzetnik, death could be physically felt and spoken to. The narrator states, "Death prowls around you" (p. 20); "Death has eased his stranglehold" (p. 36); "Death holds your life between his hands" (p. 40); "Death, your master, is now taking you to his abode" (p. 40). This literary device of referring to death as an omnipresent entity – not merely as a literary personification – enhances the feeling of its immediacy and its omnipotent presence. It helps the reader grasp the author's perception of the essence of the Holocaust as a unique and singular event.

---

9. See discussion on this subject in the chapter on Elie Wiesel.

Ka-tzetnik's way to relate a unique aspect of the concentration camp experience is done by imbedding a certain tone in his story. It is the overall tone of paradox that registers with the reader as one of the most dominant features of the Jewish catastrophe. Through an understanding of the centrality of the paradox in the Holocaust, the reader gets a unique insight into the experience of atrocity where death has paradoxically become a symbol for life. The paradox abounds as the people of Metropoli, the narrator's city, are instructed to dig their own graves, and the more they dig the longer they stay alive: "'As long as your hands keep digging [your grave] – you live!...'
"'Dig and stay alive!'" (p. 23).
Or:
The old people marching to their death know that "their going spells life for those left behind in the ghetto" (p. 29).

Ka-tzetnik's particular style of portraying the Holocaust experience is best demonstrated in the second chapter, "The Men of Metropoli." It depicts the first encounter with death as a group of Jews is ordered to dig a pit which is nothing else but a mass grave. Significantly, chapter subtitles in the original Hebrew version of the book are designated as phases in a numerical order, each chapter representing a phase in the Holocaust.[10] The reader is impressed by the fact that phase one – the digging of the pit – occurs without any warning. The omission of a detailed background being quite outstanding, it is indeed the author's way of representing the Holocaust as a sudden, illogical, senseless event. The literary components are so structured as to reflect a general concept of the historical Holocaust, namely, the fact that most Jews confronted with the situation were totally unprepared, as were the people of Metropoli.

Selective Reality

Reality as presented by the narrator is selective; it is narrowed down to the elements, to the essentials of existence. Thus, the first word in the second chapter is *Earth*. The sentence, too, is stripped to its bare essential, the subject. The lack of a verb here, as well as in many other sentences throughout the book, signifies the passivity of reality: "Naked march into the night" (p. 39); "Backs. Backs and eyes–" (p. 49); "A cataract of yellow, dried bones" (p. 71); "Rows. Naked rows" (p. 90). The tendency to deprive the scene of any unnecessary description – adjectives being a rarity in the book – helps in stripping reality as well. Similarly, human experience as depicted by the

---

10. In the English edition, the table of contents has the title 'Phases,' but each chapter is not numbered as a phase in a consecutive number, unlike the original Hebrew.

narrator is limited to the essentials: food, rollcall, curfew, cruel punishment, prayer, and death.

The tone employed here, as elsewhere, is ironic. The ground – "earth" – is the private property of a Jewish family. As it turns out, the pit dug in the earth epitomizes, at the outset, the common fate of the Jews in the Holocaust. The scenes depict the atrocity of extermination, showing the sadism, inhumanity, and dishonesty of the Nazis incorporated with their alleged cultural traits, namely cleanliness, orderliness, mechanical performance of duty, and accuracy of reporting the results of their hideous acts. The atrocity is performed in broad daylight, as the sun shines unashamedly. The narrator enacts a symbolic struggle between the atrocity and the sun's shining: "With every thrust of your spade – you bury the sun in the earth. But with every shovelful of sod tossed away, the sun floats up once more–[.] Brighter than ever" (p. 17). For the citizens of Metropoli are silent witnesses to the atrocity carried out in broad daylight.

The author chose the sun to function as a leitmotif, relating the prologue to the epilogue, and serving as a cementing bond between the prologue, the pre-Holocaust events, and the beginning of the war in chapter one. Subsequently, chapters two, three, and four, depicting the transports of the old and the young, and later of all the inhabitants of the ghetto, have both day and night scenes in them. The sun is playing the same role as before. As the scene shifts to Auschwitz, night reigns supreme. It is cited as "Midnight silence of Auschwitz" (p. 39) or "Night-of-Auschwitz" (p. 52).

The sun reappears in the Auschwitz reality as "the naked skull of the sun" (p. 80), more than ever reflecting the state of the inmates at the concentration camp. The sun is portrayed in its setting, indeed, the sunset of humanity, as "the bottom strands of the barbed-wire dykes bathe in a pool of blood. A day dies in Auschwitz" (p. 80). The earlier chapter on the narrator's city of Metropoli also presents this notion as "a city sunk into the bottom of a luminous sea" (p. 23), namely, a civilization in decline, a modern-day Atlantis. Only once more would the sun appear in all its glory and brightness; it happens, ironically, as the end draws near, in line to the crematorium. "It's bright out. Brilliant light. Suddenly you see a sky" (p. 91). The English translation loses the religious subtleties inherent in the original Hebrew text. For the author is using the word *Zohar* (Hebrew meaning "brilliance"), in the context of *Shamayim* (Hebrew meaniong "sky"), thus alluding to the memorial prayer, "*El Male Rahamim*."[11] The sun foreshadows the inmates' departure – and their demise.... Concurrently, this brightness, *Zohar* in Hebrew, carries with it a transcendental revelation alluding also to the Kabbalistic book of *Zohar*. The narrator expounds: "Until this moment nobody knew that in

---

11.   The Memorial Prayer reads: "*El male rahamim [...] kezohar haraki'a mazhirim*," having *zohar* (brilliance) and *raki'a* (sky) in the same sentence.

Auschwitz there is sky" (*Shamayim*: Hebrew meaning also "heavens"; p. 91).[12] And he goes on saying: "Only now, at final rollcall, it has disclosed itself to the eye. At the very last moment" (p. 91). Ironically, heavens reveal their existence in line to the crematorium....

This heavenly body is employed as a powerful metaphor at the concluding scenes of liberation. The Ka-tzetnik summarizes the total image of the sun and its disappearance as symbol of the Holocaust and his experience at the concentration camp referring to it as "the eclipse of his world's sun [...] the eclipse of his life's sun" (p. 115).

Stars and Sparks

The dominant figure of the sun is replaced by the equally forceful image of the stars in the dominion of night as the "Night-of-Auschwitz" (p. 52) prevails. As conceptualized by the author, the stars, like the sun, are reflecting the mundane, down-to-earth reality in all its gruesomeness:

Over your head vaults a star-sprinkled sky, and before your eyes a smokestack thrusts skyward. Thick, fatty smoke gushes out. Sparks beyond count. Sparks scatter and flash across the starry sky, mingle with the stars, and you cannot tell whose light is the brighter (p. 40).

Smoke, too, is a symbol of the Holocaust here and elsewhere in the literature. Its color is blue (p. 94) as is the color of the Ka-Tzet number on the narrator's forearm, which – the narrator describes – resembles a blue river of Jewish experience during the Holocaust (pp. 118–119). The author's metaphor of the river may allude to the well-known episode told in *The Ethics of the Fathers (Pirkei Avot)* of the sage Hillel walking by a river. Seeing a skull [of a highway robber] floating on it, he said: "For drowning others thou wast drowned."[13] Of course, this phrase evokes the notion of retribution. As will be discussed in a subsequent chapter, other Hebrew writers, such as Yehuda Amichai, intensified this saying to a major concept of the Holocaust experience.[14]

In the context of stars and sparks, one should note another significant literary device employed in Ka-tzetnik's writings. It is especially discernible through his use of the Hebrew language in the original work. The narrator designates those stars and sparks, as described in the above scene, to serve as leitmotifs throughout the book. They are charged with meaningful biblical allusions. In so doing, the author adds historical and religious depths to the meaning and significance of the Shoah in the history of the Jewish people. The depiction of the stars clearly refers to the biblical covenant between God and

---

12. Hebrew edition: *Kochav Ha'efer*, p. 84.
13. *Pirkei Avot*, chapter 2, v. 6 [Hebrew].
14. Yehuda Amichai uses this allusion in his novel *Not of This Time, Not of this Place* (New York, 1968), see later chapter.

Abraham, cited as follows: "He took him outside and said, 'Look toward heaven and count the stars, if you are able to count them.' And He added: 'So shall your offspring be'" (*Genesis* 15:5). The author portrays the reality of the Holocaust by describing the numberless smoke sparks that replace the promised numberless stars, which symbolize the eternity of the Hebrew people. Ironically, and quite painfully, these sparks represent the actual doom of the Jewish people in the Holocaust. As "Sparks slip out of the smokestack" – "Stars vanish" (p. 41). These two phenomena of the Holocaust are directly connected to the disappearance of "human language" (p. 41), as previously mentioned.

The Star which appears in the original title of the book was given the English rendering of "Star Eternal." It is an erroneous, perhaps ironic, representation of the original "*Kochav Ha'efer*," namely, "Star of Ash(es)," a title which is more meaningful.

Mound of Ash

For it is the author's intention to enhance the symbol of the ashes as a major concept of the Holocaust not only as part of the concentration camp experience which is also used by other writers, such as Elie Wiesel,[15] but indeed as a dominant feature of the post-Holocaust experience. Liberated after the war, the Ka-tzet faces the crematorium – and his past, and he says:

"No one inside, no one outside. All are here now – in the mound of ash.

"'Dear ones! My darlings! This is the liberation! – –'

"He flung himself upon them. Took them in his arms. Held them tight. He was lying on the mound, his arms deep, deep in ash" (p. 112).

This mound of ash becomes a biblical archetypal guide, which is intended "to point out his way" (p. 112). The use of the Hebrew phrase *Lanhoto hadarech* (meaning "to point out his way") in the original Hebrew edition is a direct borrowing from the biblical reference to the divine guidance: "The Lord went before them, in a pillar of cloud by day to guide them along the way" (*Exodus* 13:21).

To the survivor, the divine guidance is replaced by the memory of those who were exterminated in the concentration camps. He says: "– I vow on you[r] ash embraced in my arms, to be a voice unto you [...] I will not cease to tell of you even unto the last whisper of my breath" (p. 113). Similar vows appear in other writings on the Holocaust. One remembers Elie Wiesel's similar utterances in *Night*: "Never shall I forget."[16]

---

15. Elie Wiesel, *Night* (Avon Books, New York: 1969), p. 79; Bantham edition: p. 65. See the chapter on Wiesel.

16. Wiesel, *Night*, Avon Books, p. 44; Bantham edition: p. 32. See the chapter on Wiesel.

Other biblical allusions abound in his writing and are related to Ka-tzetnik's conceptualization of the Shoah. While not referred to directly, yet existing in the backdrop as a subconscious phenomenon, the biblical covenant with the Hebrew people emerges through a variety of biblical allusions in their caustic contradictions. As previously seen, stars – the symbol of the covenant – become ashes in the Holocaust. This major concept of the Jewish catastrophe as presented from a meaningful, historical point of view, is enhanced by a similar expression which becomes the title of a chapter. It is "Covenant Between the Crumbs," a parody of the Covenant Between the Pieces (*Genesis* ch. 15), which has both doom yet also a promised salvation in it. It is related to the promise of land and people to Abraham. Yet in the context of the Holocaust, the ironic covenant is one of separation between the lover and his beloved, with nothing to hope for except the token expression of love. One notes under these circumstances the disappearance of the stars: "See! These are no stars twinkling above our heads. They are stray sparks, from the crematorium chimney..." (p. 89). The star of ashes emerges as the most authentic symbol of the Holocaust.

Ka-tzetnik's style tends to be repetitious; thus, it adds a semblance of poetry to the book. It looks as though the English edition, unlike the original Hebrew, was trying to attribute some poetic format to the book by having the text printed in uneven, unjustified lines. By so doing, the publisher of the English edition ostensibly ignored Adorno's well-known statement: "To write poetry after Auschwitz is barbaric."[17]

Perception of Reality

More importantly, the continuous repetition seems to reflect the monotony of life, or rather the monotony of death, in the Holocaust experience. The monotonous rhythm reflects the narrator's struggle in the attempt to recapture events, situations, scenes, and places in order to present them authentically. A phrase may be repeated several times in a given chapter. For example, the phrase "Isolation Block" is repeated three times (pp. 102–103), or "Eyes" some five times (pp. 50–52).

This device of repetition becomes, at times, a very sophisticated way in which reality is conceptualized and presented by Ka-tzetnik. Note the following examples:
"Backs.
"Backs and eyes–" (p. 49);

---

17. Theodor W. Adorno, *Noten zur Literatur, Gesammelte Schriften*, II (Frankfurt A/M, 1974), S. 422: "Nach Auschwitz noch Lyric zu schreiben, sei barbarisch." Adorno's book has been translated into English. See *Notes to Literature*, II (New York, 1992), pp. 87–88, chapter on "Commitment."

Or:
    "Rows.
    "Naked rows.
    "Naked yellow skeletons" (p. 90).
Through this use of repetitive phrases, the narrator presents a linear perception of reality, somewhat limited in scope, depth, and breadth. Field of vision, too, is narrow. Ability to grasp simultaneous or complex components is curtailed. It is a tired outlook, primitive in nature, which concentrates on the bare essentials as does the actual Holocaust experience itself. This portrayal of a distorted reality is part of an overall endeavor to relate the reality of the Shoah to the reader.

Perception and portrayal of people are also linear and limited. The narrator refers to people just by citing parts of their bodies: eyes, legs, backs, and necks. There is no concept of the person as an individual nor a portrayal of one's personality except as a member of a group identified only by the part of the body which the group has in common. It is a very powerful way of delineating the experience of the World War II calamity in Europe. In a more subtle way, it is a cruel and sardonic, yet authentic, foreshadowing of the tragic fate of these victims in the Holocaust. Anyone who saw a highly moving documentary film such as *Night and Fog*[18] would never forget the visual trauma and emotional impact of such scenes as the piles of skulls or hair displayed in a macabre, satanic way. (Ka-tzetnik uses such scenes in the final chapter on reparations, pp. 120–126.) They utterly distort reality as we know it and introduce us into the reality of *l'univers concentrationnaire*, the reality of the concentration camp. It is a reality of a macabre display of human organs and of life whose terrifying description defies human imagination. It is, as Langer puts it, the disfiguration of empirical reality.[19]

The eyes and legs become leitmotifs in the book, recurring as symbols of atrocity (pp. 21, 51), although in a less impressive way than the eyes are used by Kosinski in *The Painted Bird*.[20]

While Ka-tzetnik's book on the Holocaust does have its limitations and shortcomings, it is nevertheless very effective in relating the Holocaust experience to the reader and to the student of the literary expression of the Holocaust. To the latter, this book serves as a fascinating study – if one is permitted to use this improper term – of the art of atrocity. Ka-tzetnik struggles with his own conceptualization of the Holocaust, and he perceives it and portrays it as only an author who experienced the atrocities on his own self would.

---

18. *Nait et Brouillard* [Night and Fog], Alain Resnais, director, filmed in 1955.
19. Langer, *The Holocaust and the Literary Imagination*, pp. 2–3.
20. See note 8 above, and the relevant chapter on Kosinski.

Chapter 5
Jerzy Kosinski: *The Painted Bird* –
The Risk of Metaphor

"Perhaps nowhere in modern fiction – certainly not in the literature of atrocity – is [...the] conception of metaphor as an instrument of dehumanization more effectively exploited than in Jerzy Kosinski's *The Painted Bird*," wrote Lawrence Langer in his *The Holocaust and the Literary Imagination*. "One wanders through its pages with sensations ranging from awe to revulsion, much as Dante must have felt when introduced by Virgil to the bizarre horrors of Hell."[1]

It is this aspect of *The Painted Bird* that created the controversy about Kosinski's book. Continued Langer, "In Kosinski's hands metaphor is an instrument of desecration, a tool of the imagination shaping a world populated by creatures whose values coincide with those of Auschwitz, as if no other had ever existed. In such a world man appears as a fugitive from all but his animal origins."[2]

The metaphor is anchored in a harsh reality "in the most backward part of Eastern Europe" (p. 2 in the Bantam Books edition; p. 4, in the Grove Press edition).[3]

As described in the preface which lays out the backdrop to Kosinski's novel, "In the first weeks of World War II, in the fall of 1939, a six-year-old

---

1. Lawrence L. Langer, *The Holocaust and the Literary Imagination* (New Haven, 1975), pp. 166–167.
2. *Ibid.*, p. 167.
3. Jerzy Kosinski, *The Painted Bird* (Boston: Bantam Books, 1975); (New York: Grove Books, 1995). Pagination will be marked likewise in the rest of the chapter.

boy from a large city in Eastern Europe was sent by his parents, like thousands of other children, to the shelter of a distant village" (p. 1; 3). The boy was transplanted into an alien environment with which he was not acquainted. It was a village that has been neglected for centuries, totally detached from the rest of Europe, or for that matter from the rest of civilization. The villagers were ignorant, brutal, and superstitious; the only law "was the traditional right of the stronger and wealthier over the weaker and poorer" (p. 2; 4). The boy's identity was not spelled out clearly: he had olive skin, dark hair, and black eyes, and was considered either "a Gypsy or Jewish stray," and did not speak the dialect of the local peasants.

Thus, he was completely estranged from his parents, detached from his roots, and in effect totally disconnected from his surroundings. As the novel unfolds the boy tells his impressions of the transition in first person: "But this past of mine was rapidly turning into an illusion like one of my old nanny's incredible fables" (p. 8; 10). The reality was even more incredible than these fables, and perhaps this raw reality turned out to be a fable of another reality, as suggested by the concept of the metaphor.

His alienation and detachment is epitomized by a lack of communication with the peasants or among them; there is very little dialogue in the novel. It is demonstrated in the scene of the runaway boy returning to the carpenter who in turn kicks him away "without a word and calmly continued preparing the sack" (p. 54; 62).

The protagonist is alienated from the peasants by his appearance, being Gypsy or Jewish, and is placed in a reality that is unfamiliar to him or to the readers and seems to be remote in time and place. Even though the preface places the story in Eastern Europe at the beginning of the war, as the novel unfolds the readers cannot be certain about this information, and they keep asking themselves when and where does the story take place. Is it in the Middle Ages or in the twentieth century, the so-called 'enlightened' century?

In order to portray this troubling reality, Kosinski takes his nameless protagonist, as if in a picaresque novel, from place to place, from master to master, and from one situation to another. All these transitions create the reality of atrocity, where the set of values, beliefs, ethics, and ethos are diametrically different from the ones known and acceptable in civilized society. The sum total of the boy's experiences, trials, and tribulations could not but affect a traumatic shock on the reader, as indeed intended by the author.

One may attempt to classify the boy's experiences with terms such as *barbaric, primitive, superstitious, cruel, hateful, heinous,* or *monstrous,* but these terms are pale when compared to the events themselves, as told by Kosinski.

An Act of Initiation into Savagery

What type of experiences does Kosinski invent in order to form his kind of reality and how does he describe them? One exemplary experience described in detail is a scene which seems to be an act of initiation into nature as the boy is 'planted' into the ground in order to heal him from his high fever. Olga dug a deep pit, ordered him to take off his clothes and get into the pit, and then pushed the earth back into the pit. "I was buried up to my neck," the boy recounts the experience. "Thus planted in the cold earth, my body cooled completely in a few moments, like the root of a wilting weed. I lost all awareness. Like an abandoned head of cabbage, I became part of the great field" (pp. 19–20; 23).

In this macabre act of trying to cure him of high fever, the boy is now becoming part of nature as he is united physically with Mother Earth; but he is in effect being buried alive. It is portrayed as a meaningful act of the boy's metamorphosis into the 'other' reality. In this 'rite of passage' the boy loses his humanity and feels that he became a plant with its head moving toward the sun. He is depicted in an ambiguous state of being a living dead as he imagines ants and cockroaches threatening to eat out his thoughts. Then the ravens peck at his head as if he were already dead. And indeed it is this concept that Kosinski is trying to impart. It is a parody on the act of initiation into nature, but that primordial nature is far from being pure and pristine; it is tainted by these human beings into savagery and cruelty

Finally, he feels that "I was myself now a bird" (p. 22; 25), a statement that foreshadows the scene of the painted bird and its meaning. The metamorphosis of man into animal or bird is tied to that central metaphor of the novel – the painted bird.

The Painted Bird: Bird of Another Feather

The metaphor of the painted bird is developed early in the novel as Leech the bird hunter teaches the boy about the origins of birds. Lekh regards the cuckoos "as people turned into birds – noblemen, begging God in vain to turn them back into humans" (p. 39; 45). He teaches the boy that "a man should always watch birds carefully and draw conclusions from their behavior" (p. 39; 46).

Providing folklore motifs as the basis for the painted bird, Kosinski extends the story to a symbolic metaphor, leading to the scene in which Lekh is the major player painting the bird. Lekh selected a bird, painted its body and wings with very colorful paint, and then released the bird among the same species. The painted bird was trying to join the brown flock, but the birds "were confounded." Then "The painted bird circled from one end of the flock to the other, vainly trying to convince its kin that it was one of them. But, dazzled by its brilliant colors, they flew around it" (p. 44; 51). First the birds rejected it because of its external appearance, even though it was one of them, and then attacked it savagely, pecking out its eyes and eventually killing it.

The description is vivid; it is the epitome of parricide, a cruel killing perpetrated by the same species just because of a superficial external difference. The victim cannot understand the reason for the attack, and the more it attempts to come closer to the group of ravens, the worse off it is, until it finally brings itself to its own demise.

This depiction of kinsmen cruelty becomes a foreshadowing expression of the main story in the novel: the story of a boy who was different in the color of his skin, hair, and eyes from the surrounding people, and thus was rejected by them. The people could not and would not recognize him as one of them because they consider him as the 'other.' Of course, the metaphor has a dual meaning that extends beyond the boy in the story to the essential meaning of the Holocaust: rejection of man, and eventually causing his annihilation, just because of his different looks, outlook, culture, or religious practices. Very clearly, Kosinski selected words in the depiction of the birds' cruelty to imply a human context, such as, "The painted bird circled from one end of the flock to the other, vainly trying to convince its kin that it was one of them" (p. 44; 51).[4]

Cruelty as a Value

It is this kind of cruelty that becomes part of the laws of nature, indeed the laws of the reality described in these pages. These savage cruelties are depicted repeatedly in many scenes in the novel to the point of becoming this reality's normality.

To understand Kosinski's way of depicting atrocities, of which there are many, it will be worthwhile to examine one of the most gruesome atrocities enacted in the novel. It is the scene in which the miller gouges out the eyes of the plowboy, which is described very graphically: As the miller held the boy in his hands,

[...]with a rapid movement such as women use to gouge out the rotten spots while peeling potatoes, he plunged the spoon into one of the boy's eyes and twisted it.

The eye sprang out of his face like a yolk from a broken egg and rolled down the miller's hand onto the floor. The plowboy howled and shrieked, but the miller's hold kept him pinned against the wall. Then

---

4.   A similar technique of applying human terms to animal's cruelty is found in the episode with the storks (p. 38; 44. See below).

the blood-covered spoon plunged into the other eye, which sprang out even faster. For a moment the eye rested on the boy's cheek as if uncertain what to do next; then it finally tumbled down his shirt onto the floor [...] I could not believe what I had seen (pp. 32–33; 38).

Readers tend to react very negatively after reading this episode, and Kosinski addressed this matter in an interview that he gave in 1968:

I remember a woman who told me that she couldn't read the book; she reached this particular episode and couldn't go through it. When I said why, she said, the eyes are being gouged out. And I said well, there are worse things, there were worse things, there have been worse things in our reality. Have you heard of the concentration camps? Or gas chambers? And she said, gas chambers? Certainly, this I understand very well, but gouging out someone's eyes, how can you explain something like this? And this is my point. The concentration camp as such is a symbol you can live with very well. We do. It doesn't really perform any specific function. It's not as closed to us as the eyesight is. When you describe the atrocity of the concentration camp you are immediately reminding the reader that this is not his reality [...] But when you describe the eyes being gouged out, you don't make it easier for the reader, he cannot help feeling his own eyes disappearing somehow, becoming blind.[5]

This episode of the miller and the plowboy is important to understand Kosinski's working concepts in this novel, as expounded by him in that cited interview. This atrocity, too, is becoming a metaphor for the atrocities of the death camps during the Shoah. From the beginning of the novel the eyes serve as a leitmotif. The eyes of the protagonist boy were mentioned as a representation of evil, and furthermore, based on superstition, as a tool of punishment. Earlier on, the peasants were fearful of the boy's eyes, believing that he was possessed by the evil spirit.[6] Thus, the meaning of such an atrocity enacted as punishment on the plowboy whom the miller suspects of 'lusting' for his wife.

The episode is loaded with intense depiction of atrocity in a most graphic way. It is the human eye that projects feelings, wisdom or stupidity, anger or sorrow, which is now removed in this act. Compared to a yoke of an egg, the scene is brought closer to the reader's comprehension with its

---

5.   Quoted by Langer, *The Holocaust and the Literary Imagination*, pp. 174–175.

6.   *The Painted Bird*, p. 14; 17: "I stared at a few of them straight in the eye, and they would rapidly avert their eyes or spit three times and drop their gaze"; p. 16; 20: "She called me the Black One. From her I learned for the first time that I was possessed by an evil spirit [....] Such a person as I, [...] could be recognized by his bewitched black eyes [....] Hence, Olga declared, I could stare at other people and unknowingly cast a spell over them."

feeling of disgust and also as an irreversible act. The depiction is intensified as the first-person narrator describes the cats playing with the eyes, while the eyes stare at him until the miller finally squashed the eyeballs with his heavy boots (pp. 33–34; 38–39).

The protagonist later touches his own eyes from time to time to be sure that they are intact, as would the reader, perhaps, do as well.

More Cruelties: The Epitome of Life Is Death

Another in the series of graphic depictions is the shocking scene of the carpenter who, while threatening the boy's life, was pushed into a well and devoured by waves of rats. It is a horrible depiction in slow motion as viewed through the boy's eyes:

The massive body of the carpenter was only partly visible. His face and half of his arms were lost under the surface of the sea of rats, and wave after wave of rats was scrambling over his belly and legs. The man completely disappeared, and the sea of rats churned even more violently [...]. The animals now fought for access to the body – panting, twitching their tails, their teeth gleaming under their half-open snouts (p. 55; 63).

This gruesome scene ends with the depiction of the carpenter's "bony hand with bony spreadeagled fingers" rising, followed by his entire arm. Then "the entire bluish-white skeleton of the carpenter, partly defleshed and partly covered with shreds of reddish skin and gray clothing," was thrust to the surface. When it came back again to the surface "it was a completely bare skeleton" (pp. 55–56; 64). It is a depiction that presents a horrific scene of life turning into death, of a body turning into a skeleton, in a macabre process, while the distinction between the two states of life and death is ambiguous.

As in similar episodes, the author's intent is to duplicate a reality to which the reader is totally alienated; it is a reality where the epitome of life is in effect death, and where the distinction between the two is completely obliterated, resorting to the overall premise that alludes to the reality of the death camps. This savagery is part of the novel's reality with its mirror-image reality, as depicted in these pages.

This notion of an alien reality has been demonstrated from the beginning of the novel. It is engulfing the whole scope of the story's 'universe.' It encompasses bird's cruelty to bird: exemplified by the black bird of prey attacking a pigeon that joined a flock of chicks, was estranged from them, and did not have the ability to escape (p. 4; 6). This was a foreshadowing of the painted bird metaphor. Similarly, the storks' cruelty toward one of their own which had the misfortune of having Lekh place a goose egg with her other stork eggs. When the chicks hatched "Father Stork charged his wife with adultery and wanted to kill the bastard chick." The storks finally killed "the faithless wife" (p. 38; 44). So did the rats eventually kill each other (p. 53; 61).

Cruelty of animal to man is exemplified in the episode of the carpenter and the rats, discussed above.

And so is the savagery of man to animal: the village boys catch a squirrel who befriended the boy and burn it alive (pp. 5–6; 7–8); also, the rabbit that was running with half the skin off its body and then was killed by Makar, who earlier had copulated with it (pp. 132–133; 149–150).

Cruelty of man to man is rampant: The miller beats his wife; the peasants raped Ludmila when she was young; and so on: women kill another woman, Ludmila; peasants let the Jewish boy who was thrown off the train die and took his clothes; additionally, there are rape, bestiality, castration, torture. The whole litany of savage cruelty and bestiality may be found right here in the novel.

This leads to a major question about the overall concept of this book and the reluctance of many readers to accept it as just a metaphor for the Holocaust. Langer agrees that the metaphors serve as means of expressing the inexpressible.[7] However, to some people many of these depictions border with pornography. The depictions are so graphic that they are overwhelming. They are crude in their vulgarity, and they are repulsive and revulsive to such an extent that their use defeats the author's purpose. Reading Appelfeld, Primo Levi, and Wiesel gives the reader more insights about the Holocaust than Kosinski's metaphors of cruelties. Nevertheless, some of the metaphors which do not border with the pornographic, such as the painted bird, are very powerful.

Quest for Meaning: Understand the Ruling Pattern of the World

While metaphor plays a major role in Kosinski's novel, the author aims to convey another notion related to the world of his depiction. As the boy goes on his cavalcade into the world of atrocities, he attempts to find some reason for the atrocities and punishments and some explanation for his peculiar situation and for the governing rules of the world. It is the author's delineation of the quest for meaning.

First, the boy looks for the answer to his miseries and misfortunes in magic as he examines the belief in justice. That justice rules the world is exemplified in the novel by the superstitious belief regarding a murder. Accordingly, blood stains "testifying to the crime" would eventually "draw the murderer back to the spot against his will and lead to his death." The stains would not be wiped out by rain or fire, and that even after many

---

7.   Langer, *The Holocaust and the Literary Imagination*, p. 172.

years, "the victim punished the executioner, and justice prevailed" (pp. 75–77; 87–88).

Unsatisfied, the boy then looks for the explanation to his misery and the alien environment which confronts him in Christianity. He reaches the conclusion that his problems could be solved through prayers and indulgences (p. 111; 125).

The boy concludes that "the ruling pattern of the world" rewards those who pray first to earn and collect more days of indulgencies. Thus he stops blaming other people for his misfortunes and just blames himself. He now realizes that there is order and justice in the world; he feels that he has found "the governing principle of the world of people, animals and events": "One had only to recite prayers" (p. 111; 126), and he devotes his entire time to praying (p. 112; 127). It turns out to be a satire on praying and religious belief.

The religious solution for the ruling pattern in the world still leaves an open question in his mind. He questions, from a child's perspective, why does God need to be compensated by having so many Jews killed as punishment for killing his son. He reaches the conclusion that "Perhaps the world would soon become one vast incinerator for burning people. Had not the priest said that all were doomed to perish" (p. 89; 101).

Parody of Christianity

While still in the Christian phase of his quest for the ruling pattern of the world, the boy begins to recite prayers and earn days of indulgence for his "heavenly account" (p. 112; 127). But apparently the prayers did not help him. Garbos hangs him from the ceiling, an act that seems to parody the crucifixion (p. 115; 131). On Corpus Christi, a day on which "the bodily presence of the Son of God would make itself felt in the church," the boy, having accumulated many prayers, enters the church to act as an altar boy (p. 120; 135). What ensues is again a parody reenactment of Jesus entering into Jerusalem, as the peasants scourge him with osier branches and horsewhips (p. 121; 136). Concurrently, the boy notices that the replica of the body of crucified Jesus seemed almost lifelike, his eyes looking downward below the altar in silence (p. 123; 138). Finally, the boy is thrown into a pit of manure filth, in a parody of baptism (p. 124; 139).

It is at this juncture that the boy loses his voice. He reasons that there is a greater force with which he did not manage to communicate that commands his destiny. And it is not God or his saints who inflicted these punishments on him (p. 126; 141). The answers to the boy's misery or to the order of the world are not found in the church and its faith as practiced by these peasants. Losing his voice, he thus loses any semblance of humanity. His muteness, the inability to talk, represents the animalistic state of civilization. But toward the end, the boy regains his voice, and apparently there is a glimpse of hope.

The boy's other theories of the ruling patterns are the powers of Satan (p. 137; 154) and Stalin (ch. 16). However, he did not find the definite answer in any of those, and neither does the reader.

The Author's Own Interpretation

So, what is *The Painted Bird* all about?

Kosinski provided his own interpretation in his *Notes of the Author on The Painted Bird.*[8] He writes:

THE PAINTED BIRD, then, could be the author's vision of himself as a child, a *vision*, not an examination, or a revisitation of childhood. This vision, this search for something lost, can only be conducted in the metaphor through which the unconscious most easily manifests itself, and toward which the unconscious most naturally navigates. The locale and the setting are likewise metaphorical, for the whole journey could actually have taken place in the mind. Just as the setting is metaphorical, so do the characters become archetypes, symbols of things equally felt and equally intangible, the symbols though, being doubly real – since they are the expression of the things they represent.

The readers, then, should ask themselves whether the explanation regarding this metaphorical voyage of the mind works. Do the extreme descriptions of bestiality to the point of pornography help bring the reader any closer to the understanding of the Holocaust, its unique ideological background, and its meaning to Western civilization, or just the reverse?

The Primordial World vis-à-vis
Modern Civilization that Brought about the Holocaust

Kosinski employs symbols in the novel in a clear and vivid way so that the reader can decipher and even visualize them. First and foremost is the forest where the novel takes place. It is indeed the primordial venue of human primitive existence, perhaps even in pre-civilization time. The narrator continuously alludes to it as he says that "The forest became increasingly dense and forbidding. [...] The linden trees [...] according to Lekh, remembered the very beginnings of the human race" (p. 40; 47).

Through the depiction of Lekh the reader gets a glimpse into that primitive milieu. Lekh considers Ludmila "to belong to that pagan, primitive kingdom of birds and forests where everything was infinitely

---

8. Jerzy Konsinki, *Notes of the Author on The Painted Bird* (New York, 1967), pp. 13–14.

abundant, wild, blooming, and royal in its perpetual decay, death and rebirth; illicit and clashing with the human world" (p. 42; 49).

This depiction of the primordial forest changes all of a sudden upon an occurrence that is related to the Holocaust, and thus is of utmost importance to the understanding of Kosinski's work: "The symphony of the forest was broken only by the puffing of a locomotive, the rattle of cars, the grinding of the brakes. People stood still, looking toward the tracks. The birds grew silent, the owl drew deeper into its hole" (p. 88; 100). As the narrative goes on to depict the horrors of the war, there is immediately a complete reversal of the depiction of the forest and its inhabitants. Suddenly the forest becomes tranquil, quiet, ideal, temporarily though – almost an antithesis to the war and the Holocaust.

It is the author's comment about the enormous and unparalleled atrocity of the Holocaust as compared to the reality depicted in the novel. The peasants and their way of life are not divorced from the Holocaust. As a matter of fact, the novel relates that the peasants are aware of the transportation of Jews in cattle cars and their fate in the gas chambers. They listen to the stories about the Jews and comment that it was "the Lord's punishment" that they deserved long ago

ever since they crucified Christ. God never forgot. [...] Now the Lord was using the Germans as His instrument of justice. The Jews were to be denied the privilege of a natural death. They had to perish by fire, suffering the torments of hell here on earth. They were being justly punished for the shameful crimes of their ancestors, for refuting the only True Faith, for mercilessly killing Christian babies and drinking their blood (pp. 84–85; 96).

Kosinski displays classical anti-Semitism and medieval blood libels as associated with these peasants' established beliefs. The peasants further put their thoughts into practice as reported by the boy: "After each train had passed I saw whole battalions of ghosts with evil, vengeful faces coming into the world. The peasants said the smoke from the crematories went straight to heaven, laying a soft carpet at God's feet" (p. 89; 101). Then the narrative goes on to describe how the peasants let the Jewish boy, who was thrown out of the train so he might be rescued, die, and later describes the horrid rape of a little Jewish girl who was found wandering by one of the peasants, Rainbow, who mutilated her body in this act (pp. 92–93; 105–106).

It is here that the peasants are no longer 'imagined' metaphors; they become part of the Holocaust, actively engaged in annihilating Jews. Their words and deeds are the author's realistic statements about classical, religious anti-Semitism of the most primitive nature.

At the end, the boy was found by his parents and he regained his speech. But it "mattered little if one was mute; people did not understand one another anyway" (p. 212; 233). Is there a glimpse of hope? Langer thinks not.[9] Yet, the author finishes his novel saying that "speech was now mine and that it did not intend to escape" (p. 213; 234).

---

9.   Langer, *The Holocaust and the Literary Imagination*, p. 190.

After the Holocaust –
Experience From Without

Chapter 6
Hanoch Bartov: A Late Encounter with the Holocaust – Paradigms, Rhythms, and Concepts in *The Brigade*

One may question whether Bartov's *The Brigade* could, and should, be considered as a Holocaust novel. If by "Holocaust literature" we mean imaginative writing about the experience of the Holocaust, it is apparent that this novel does not deal directly with the Holocaust experience. Indeed, the original title of the novel in Hebrew, *Pitz'ei Bagrut* ("acnes," or "wounds of maturity"), which was published in 1965, will testify to that. The original title refers to the process of maturing which the teenager-protagonist undergoes. The title in the English edition, published in 1968, is *The Brigade*, referring to the Jewish Brigade formed toward the end of World War II as part of the British army.[1]

While not purported to be a depiction of the Holocaust experience, the novel describes the experiences of a young Palestinian Jew and his encounters with the post-Holocaust situation in Europe at the end of the war and the period immediately afterwards.

It is important to note that the author does not even place his protagonist at the scenes of the Holocaust, but only lets him come close to them. Thus, the locales are Italy, Austria, and Germany, but nowhere at the actual sites of the atrocities. The Jewish soldiers, members of the Brigade, come close to a concentration camp only once, passing by it in shock. Likewise, the time in which events occur in the novel is mostly after the war. In other words, the author did not undertake to write a Holocaust novel, and he made sure that his intention would not be misinterpreted as

---

1.   Hanoch Bartov, *Pitz'ei Bagrut* [Acnes; Wounds of Maturity] (Tel Aviv, 1965) [Hebrew]; Hanoch Bartov, *The Brigade* (Philadelphia, 1968).

such. He is true to his own experience, that of an Israeli- (or Palestinian-) born Sabra who did not have a direct contact with the Holocaust.[2]

This tendency on the part of the Israeli writers of the 1948 generation to treat the Holocaust from some distance, as actually experienced by these writers, has already been noted by Gershon Shaked.[3] As will be discussed in a following chapter, Yehuda Amichai's novel *Not of This Time, Not of This Place* is one such attempt to search one's own identity and one's lost childhood in relation to the attitude toward the Holocaust. Another attempt to deal with some aspects of post-Holocaust experience is Hayim Gouri's novel, *The Chocolate Deal*, discussed in a later chapter. These works by Amichai and Gouri should be distinguished from those by Aharon Appelfeld. As mentioned previously, although Appelfeld is of the same generation of these Israeli writers, he is European born and a survivor.

The view of the Holocaust in Bartov's *The Brigade* is from the outside. The external treatment is thus one of attitude and reaction. The themes raised in this connection are those that are *related* to the Holocaust insofar as the outsiders are concerned. Some of the themes may be, in other contexts, related to the survivors as well. However, Bartov concentrates on the attitude of the onlookers as such. The themes in the novel are concerned with moral questions such as vengeance and rescue; others are related to causality topics such as religious anti-Semitism. There are also psychological themes such as the feeling of guilt, which was felt by the outsiders. Also, some general topics are related to the question of Jewish identity which are intensified as a result of the Holocaust. As a post-Holocaust novelist, the author is only marginally interested in the fate of the survivors as viewed by the Palestinian Jews.

It may be superfluous to state that in the context of a study of the literary expression of the Holocaust one may leave room for this kind of literature which attempts to present authentically a view from the outside. Similarly, it should be noted that the further we move from the event itself, the more likely we are to get the post-Holocaust emphasis in the literature pertaining to the Holocaust. One may state the obvious by saying that the Holocaust left its marks on the twentieth and twenty-first centuries, and thus it has, and it should, become the concern of every sensitive human being as we are all affected by it in one way or another. As the years go by, there is a growing, subtle awareness of the Holocaust's implication to humanity *in toto* and especially to post-Holocaust world Jewry and to Israeli Jews. Thus, the Holocaust has become directly or indirectly one of the major events related to the human condition in that century and beyond. It may be

---

2.   *Cf.* Robert Alter, *After the Tradition* (New York, 1969), p. 179.
3.   Gershon Shaked, *Gal Hadash Basiporet Ha'ivrit* [A New Wave in Hebrew Fiction] (Tel Aviv, 1971), pp. 71–72 [Hebrew].

asserted without exaggeration that to contemporary Jews the catastrophe in Europe has become a major event of historical proportion in the annals of the Jewish people. It may be equated to – and indeed exceeding – other chronicled destructions, persecutions, and attempts to annihilate Jewish communities. And definitely the Holocaust may get its historical dimensions in light of past atrocities perpetrated against the Jewish people.

With the passing years, as scholars gain more knowledge and insights into the Holocaust upon the discovery of previously unknown documents and data, it is incumbent upon the students of this event to explore it further in various related disciplines.

•

This chapter concerns itself with the study of Bartov's novel *The Brigade* as related to the Holocaust and to the imaginative literature on the Shoah.

An attempt to classify the novel in accordance with established literary genres, while a valuable task, may prove unrewarding. For one, its resemblance to a war novel is only superficial as it lacks the fanfare, the 'odor of gunpowder,' so to speak, the smoke, and the battle cry usually associated with that genre. It seems that even the descriptions of the military and military life in the novel are governed by other literary interests.

Similarly, even though the novel contains some aspects of the travelogue, the novelist employs the 'landscape' not so much for sightseeing as for guides leading, in a continuous movement, toward (but only close to) the site of the Holocaust, namely, from Italy to Germany.

The affinity with the *Bildungsroman* is perhaps stronger, as the Hebrew title implies. Nevertheless, the novel lacks the depth and breadth of, and the concentration on, its central protagonist to establish itself as such.

However, structurally one may find in the novel a basic pattern that distinguishes it from the other genres and forms. Significantly, this pattern is related to the author's overall concept of the Holocaust. In the study of the literary expression of the Holocaust experience, this pattern may shed light on the role of Holocaust literature in general.

An Encounter

The novel is structured as an encounter – both a physical and a metaphorical encounter. The various components of the story follow this fundamental structure of an encounter between the Palestinian Jews enlisted in the Jewish Brigade and the war; it is followed by an encounter with Germans, an encounter with survivors, and leading eventually to an encounter with the site of the Holocaust *after* the event. Concurrently, the protagonist, Elisha Kruk, is portrayed as experiencing an encounter of another kind – a metaphysical or spiritual encounter with himself, with his tradition, and with his Jewish identity.

Not only are ostensibly major occurrences in the novel patterned after the concept of an encounter, but so also events of seemingly less significance or less relevance to the Holocaust. These less important encounters may prove to be of greater significance upon an in-depth reading. The protagonist is made to encounter a group of black American soldiers who deem him a messenger from the Holy Land. He also encounters a survivor who turns out to be a relative of his. The group of which the protagonist is a part encounters phenomena of anti-Semitism, and so on.

Through the employment of this structure, the author could be true to himself and to his position as an outsider to the events of the Shoah. Thus, this approach may have a universal literary appeal either to the Jewish or to the non-Jewish reader, for it may reflect the author's state of mind as an individual coming to terms with the experience of the Holocaust and with the very concepts of the Holocaust from a somewhat distant stand.

This extra-Holocaust, post-Holocaust treatment of the traumatic event by Bartov does draw its strength, tragically enough, from the fact that the Western world, inclusive of world Jewry, came to realize the magnitude of the Holocaust and its lasting effects rather belatedly. Thus, the reader is made to experience the Holocaust in an authentic way: through the experience of others who, like himself, are outsiders; through a late encounter with concepts which are only remotely related to the actual atrocities, genocide, and the annihilation of the human body and spirit. Unlike such Holocaust narratives as Ka-tzetnik's *Star Eternal* and Wiesel's *Night* (see their respective chapters), Bartov's *The Brigade* does not even attempt to place its reader, or its protagonist for that matter, as temporarily an insider, to use Langer's expression.[4] The reader is constantly and permanently an outsider as are all the Brigade's soldiers in the novel.

Belatedness

Another major concept which Bartov evokes throughout his novel is of utmost importance. It is the notion of belatedness, a feeling shared by whoever studied the Holocaust. Indeed, it is a tragic belatedness that betrays a sense of helplessness and guilt. The notion of a late realization, after the event, that the whole world watched in silence as the liquidation of the Jews took place in Europe, cannot but result in pointing an accusing finger at ourselves.

---

4.   Lawrence L. Langer, *The Holocaust and the Literary Imagination* (New Haven, 1977), p. 3.

One may safely generalize that a major strength of a novel dealing with the Holocaust, either from within or from the outside of its immediate experience, must lie in the author's ability to impart a general concept of the Holocaust in its relevance to contemporary civilization.

From this perspective, this author believes that Bartov is more than merely telling a story or relating an experience. Significantly, he is portraying a state of mind, a state of humanity. He makes a comment on the condition of man and adds a footnote to the status of contemporary Judaism. The implication of the European catastrophe, as transcending the event itself, as far as human progress and the state of Western civilization and its morality are concerned, is Bartov's inherent message to the post-Holocaust world.

Bartov is aware of the fact that, to the outsider, the experience of the Holocaust is not isolated but is related to many other questions, and thus he addresses himself to some of these questions. Consequently, the Holocaust is conceptualized as an event that has ontological implications on the contemporary state of Western civilization.

Elisha Kruk – An Idealist Rebel

The Brigade centers on the personality of Elisha Kruk. Emulating the much admired figure of Pinik, his free-thinking uncle who is an antithesis of his father, Elisha rebelled against the orthodoxy of his father. An idealist, Elisha cannot stand the business-as-usual life in Palestine, where he was born, while the war is raging in Europe. He volunteers to the Jewish Brigade in order to fight the enemy.

Leaving behind him not only the mores and religious practices of his father but also his sweetheart Noga, Elisha is portrayed as being continuously tormented by the past and as being unable to cope with the present. Running away from his father's restrictive world of traditional Judaism, Elisha is nevertheless aware of the strong ties that hold him to it. He is described as being unable to engage in pleasures of the flesh, practiced unhesitatingly by his comrades-in-arms, as he struggles to maintain what he believes are his purity and morality. He is lonely even in the midst of his fellow soldiers, having an overwhelming sense of uprootedness. Being a *Talush* (Hebrew, meaning "uprooted person") and somewhat a rebelling *Maskil* (Hebrew, meaning "an enlightened person"), Elisha is characterized as undergoing similar maturing processes to the ones experienced by rebelling young Jews in previous generations. As depicted in Hebrew literature of the nineteenth century and the early part of the twentieth century, the social and psychological processes evolve around the transition from a religious way of life to the secular milieu.

Elisha's attitude toward post-Holocaust reality is expressed through his reactions to his friends, to survivors of the calamity, and to Germans and their collaborators. As questions of avenging the dead and rescuing the living survivors arise, he must face his most acute problem, namely, the essence and meaning of his Jewish identity. This confrontation crystallizes to him in the end as he finds out that he is much closer to his father's rejected world than he had imagined.

Through Elisha's activities Bartov externalizes his protagonist's spiritual yearnings. Thus Elisha's continuous quests and aimless running should be placed and may be more meaningful in a metaphysical context. What appears to be Elisha's impotence does signify his mental and spiritual weakness (ch. 4, pp. 19–26[5]). His desire to stay pure and clean (p. 18) is delineated as related to his impotence, yet significantly it externalizes his spiritual desires and his inherent stand on the question of Jewish morality.

Moreover, the first-person narrator, Elisha, is so characterized by the author as to transcend the boundaries of his own experiences. Bartov purposefully created a noticeable correspondence between Elisha and the group, the soldiers of the Jewish Brigade.

Elisha is made to experience personally some variation of what the group does. Very cleverly, the author relates the problems of the individual with the problems of the group. By so structuring his novel, Bartov intensified some of the major themes with which the novel is concerned and made them more meaningful in a general context.

Elisha's betrayal of his father's traditions foreshadows and reflects the attitude of the Jewish Brigade, as a Jewish group, toward the Jewish concept of vengeance. While there appears to be some vacillation among the group as to what stand should be taken toward vengeance, it is nevertheless Elisha's act of non-vengeance that sets the dominant tone for the whole group.

Elisha's inability to act reflects the group's eventual failure in fulfilling its desire to fight the Germans in the war or even to avenge the Jews murdered in it. The tantalizing problem of his morality is but an echo of the overall question of Jewish morality and the question of vengeance. Similarly, his inner struggle with his heritage and his father's traditions mirrors the group's struggle with its Jewish identity and its practical application to post-Holocaust reality. This dual aspect of the novel is central to its understanding.

There is yet another role for Elisha in the structure of the novel: being a central figure in the story, his experiences are portrayed by the author as paradigmatic. Bartov does not employ this literary device as used by some other Hebrew writers. As practiced by the Holocaust author, Ka-tzetnik, and

---

5. Bartov, *The Brigade*; pages listed in parentheses refer to this edition.

discussed in a previous chapter, this device enriches the novel's structure by drawing paradigmatic parallels with biblical archetypal events.[6] While occasionally referring to meaningful biblical allusions (see below), Bartov resorts to setting paradigms within the boundaries of his novel's sphere of reality.

Paradigms

The novel unfolds in the last day of the war, as the news of the Germans' surrender reaches the Jewish army and before it had the opportunity to fire a single shot at the enemy. It is not only that it highlights a major concept of Jewish historiosophy as asserted quite correctly by Hillel Weiss, namely, that the Jew is detached from the historical processes.[7] More importantly, this episode intensifies the image of the Jew as generally being inactive, pensive, and reflective. He is perceived to be an idealist rather than a realist; his attitude, according to this concept, is not political but rather philosophical. The Jew seems to be portrayed as a bystander, observer, and commentator rather than an actor and a doer. He is conceptualized as writing history (embodied in the character of Tamari, pp. 7, 245), but not as making it. It should be noted that a similar Jewish attitude toward history is an important theme in the writings of another Hebrew writer, Hazaz.[8]

Paradigmatically, the only shot fired in the war was that of a fellow volunteer, Freedberg, inflicting it upon himself as he committed suicide. Contemplating on this symbolic event, as is oftentimes done through Elisha the first-person protagonist, the consensus is "that this peculiar coincidence did not signify what we thought it did at that first terrifying moment" (p. 13). Yet the characterization of Freedberg as an archetypal figure may certainly reveal the significance of his symbolic act. Freedberg is characterized as "one of the true volunteers," whose attitude toward their mission was such that he composed a poem titled "The Army of Redeemers" and posted it on the battalion's bulletin board (p. 13). Freedberg is further typified as being a student of medieval history specializing in the history of the Roman Catholic Church (p. 14). Being a student of the relationship between Jews and Christians, a motif that emerges in the novel, Freedberg's act indeed is of importance. As is often the case with an unreliable narrator, the narrator provided information about the meaning of Freedberg's suicide which turns out to be incorrect and

---

6. See chapter on Kosinski.
7. Hillel Weiss, *Dyoqan Halohem* [Profile of the Fighter] (Ramat Gan, 1975), p. 165 [Hebrew].
8. See, for example, Hayim Hazaz, "Adam Miyisrael" [A Man of Israel] and "Haderashah" [The Sermon], in *Supurim Nivharim* [Select Stories] (Tel Aviv, 1952), pp. 149–157, 184–202 [Hebrew].

misleading, but is done so for a purpose. However, the reader is then given clear clues concerning the narrator's true position about the suicide. Thus, the narrator advises the reader, regardless of his initial ostensible position, that "surely these few superficial facts somehow had to contain some kind of explanation; why, in God's name, had it happened?" (p. 14). Leaving the possibilities unresolved, the narrator concludes: "Accident, fate or omen – we could not escape the thought that this was the morning after the war" (p. 14). The significance and meaning of the suicide is thus revealed.

Depicted as lonely as the protagonist himself, Freedberg appears to foreshadow Elisha's impotence and also the inability of the Jewish group to act in vengeance. Friedberg's suicide becomes a symbolic act for the whole group.

The discovery of the suicide is concurrent with Elisha's self-revelation, in a flashback digression, of his own inherent inability to participate in the war. As portrayed paradigmatically by Bartov, Elisha contracts "a child's disease," identified as "German measles," and at the outset is prevented from any possible action (p. 10). While this aspect of Elisha's process of maturity is being alluded to, a scene of physical defilement ("a baby who had made in his pants," p. 11) is described so as to imply his own feelings of guilt about his moral purity. ("What a degrading experience, from which I would never purify myself," is a vital sentence uttered by Elisha which is omitted in the English translation.[9]) These occurrences foreshadow the group's inability to fight in the war and similarly its own state of defilement.

Parody of a Savior and a Mission

A third paradigm which sets the scene for the whole novel occurs in an Italian pizzeria. The protagonist is perceived by a group of black American soldiers as a Christ figure who was sent "from Bethlehem to us on a mission, that he might reveal to us something of great moment" (p. 29). Elisha's religious mission is delineated as a parodic satire on the mission undertaken by the Jewish Brigade to avenge the dead Jews and to save the survivors. The tone is ironic, the style is parodic, and the presentation by Elisha is unmistakably satiric. It is not so much the mission as perceived by the black soldiers as the conceptualization by Elisha of himself as such; namely, a take off on the image of a savior.

The teaching of the man of Nazareth lies in the backdrop as a model of Christianity which has not been practiced by some Christians in Europe during the war. The Jews' attitude toward Christianity certainly plays an important role in the novel. In a long monologue, Zunenshein, one of the

---

9.   Bartov, *Pitz'ei Bagrut*, p. 15. [Hebrew].

Jewish soldiers, asserts that they were not Christians and that they could not practice the Christian doctrine of turning the other cheek. Similarly, Elisha maintains that, "We aren't Christians." He, too, would not adopt the other cheek doctrine of the New Testament but rather accept the vengeance preached and practiced in the Hebrew Bible (p. 226). However, in spite of his wishes, Elisha is unable to practice the ancient morality of the Hebrew Bible in the literal interpretation of "an eye for an eye." While rejecting the ethical practice of the other cheek, Elisha is portrayed as a messenger of his own inherent weakness. It is the result of his ambivalent attitude toward Judaism.

The parody on the preaching of the man of Nazareth conducted by the new messenger from the Holy Land is a reminder to a cynical Christian world, (albeit exceptions), of its responsibility for past religious anti-Semitism that played a role in the European Holocaust. The Holocaust is thus conceptualized as the culmination of two millennia of Christian religious persecutions of the Jews (referred to in the novel by the well-known Passion Play at Oberammergau, p. 215).

Related to this is the notion that if anyone can be regarded as close to the teaching of the man of Nazareth, it is, ironically, Elisha himself. The phenomenon of the Holocaust is held as a blunt statement on the Christians' betrayal of Jesus' original teaching.

Parallels

In addition to the structure of paradigms within the novel, there appears to exist some covert parallels tying together various segments of the novel into meaningfully connected units. The table, his father's traditional table, from which Elisha seems to be running away, emerges in two variations. One is the table at the pizzeria (p. 27) where another religious tradition, a Christian one, is being covertly criticized and rejected by Elisha. The second instance is the Sabbath table of the Hungarian Jews, consciously made analogous to his father's table (p. 92), leading the first-person narrator to a soul searching and bringing him back closer to his father's table. Realizing his estrangement from his father's religious practices, Elisha says: "How far I had traveled in the short time since I had fled my father's table" (p. 92). One is reminded of Agnon's protagonist Joseph in the short story "The Lady and the Pedlar," which may have influenced Bartov. Joseph, going astray from Judaism, finally realizes that he was destined to be doomed. He says: "God in Heaven [...] how far have I gone! If I do not return at once, I am lost."[10]

---

10. S. Y. Agnon, *Twenty One Stories* (New York, 1971), pp. 179–180. Hillel Weiss, too, sees this parallel in *Dyoqan Halohem*, p. 186 [Hebrew].

Other parallels do exist within the story between Pinik, his uncle whom Elisha first admires and then, upon discovering his corruption, detests, and his relative, the survivor Krochmal. Both are depicted as having some moral blemish or as being corrupt, and as directly or indirectly being instrumental in Elisha's search for himself. A parallel may be found between the contemporary anti-Semitic phenomena, exemplified by the old Ukrainian women (p. 88), and the classical anti-Semitism of the Passion Play at Oberammergau (p. 215).

The three major paradigms discussed are intended to set the scene for the rest of the novel. They dictate the resulting events as acted or "unacted" upon by the protagonists.

One expects to find some meaningful basis for the author's structuring a supposedly open-ended story, in which all eventualities within the reasonable scope of a given reality may occur in such a way as to abort the Brigade's mission from its very beginning. For otherwise the characters' actions would seem arbitrarily and artificially planned by the author.

Inner Rhythm of Discovery

The basis for this is to be found in an inner rhythm within the story and equally within the characters. It takes the shape of discovery or revelation on the part of the protagonists. As events unfold before the reader, they reveal to the protagonists experiencing them, and to the reader as an observer, the nature of the inherent causes lying in the foundations of the protagonists' activities. Hidden truths are ruthlessly brought into focus; they may no longer be ignored. A facade of accepted norms tumbles down as the protagonists face themselves in this act of self-discovery.

There is a deceptive appearance in the novel of moving toward the realization of a goal, be it national or personal, on the respective levels of presentation. However, this movement is actually an escape from reality, an attempt to run away from the truth. This is exemplified in Elisha's thoughts: "I had fled, fled, but had not escaped myself" (p. 22). Elisha is running away from the "hateful [...] world of [his] Father" (p. 24), from "those damn rules and regulations" (p. 35). At the same time, his fellow soldiers are immersing themselves in carnal pleasures, in an attempt to compensate themselves for their military and national frustrations.

The encounter with the experience of the Holocaust serves as a catalyst for Elisha in helping him to come to terms with his heritage. It also serves as a catalyst for the Jewish Brigade. Bartov delineates the perennial problem of Jewish identity as related to the post-Holocaust generation of young Jews who are compelled to come to grips with existential problems related to their Jewishness. In spite of their flight from their Jewish identity, and in spite of the deceptive adaption of new, non-diaspora kind of characteristics, the young Palestinian Jew is made to find his identity which is paradoxically very much similar to the ostensibly rejected identity of the *Golah* [diaspora]-Jew.

Jewish Identity

The theme of identity is central in the novel. It appears in a variety of ways and forms in order to augment the paramount issue of Elisha's identity. It seems that many of the other characters as well are having some problem with their identities. The group of Jewish soldiers is not identified as Jewish by the non-Jews (pp. 79, 82ff.). Some of them assume an identity which is not their own: Brodsky's real name is Kirschenbaum. The new Hebrew names, given to or assumed by individuals in order to signify some break with the past and an appearance of a new Israeli trait, would fit him "like tight shoes," says Brodsky-Kirschenbaum (p. 18). Commenting on the discovery of his comrade's new identity, the first-person narrator says: "a different name, a different genealogy" (p. 18). So is Esther, the Jewish nurse in the army's hospital. Having a false Aryan identity which helped her survive during the war, Esther continues to adhere to her false identity even after the war, hesitating to reclaim her own original identity now that it is safe for her to do so (p. 91).

Not only are single individuals faced with the question of their identities but so also are the whole group of Jewish soldiers. Accused of an attempted rape and robbery – to them an act of revenge – the entire company is made to undergo a degrading identification parade as two German women, claiming to have been assaulted by the Jews, attempt to *identify* their two assailants (pp. 129–132). Since the suspects have been replaced by two other soldiers, assuming temporarily false identities, the attackers are not identified by the two women. Regardless of the results, this act has been done. Bartov portrays here a very meaningful act of identification whereby the non-Jews, and in this case Germans, are made to perform an act of identifying Jews. A sense of irony prevails throughout this act. For it is not only the historic echoes that the author evokes here concerning the negative definition of a Jew (that is, he who the non-Jew defines as a Jew), but also re-enactment of the war situation – after the war.

By reversing the roles of the accuser and the accused after the war, Bartov also creates a distortion of post-Holocaust reality. Thus, through this literary device of the distortion of reality the author continues the task undertaken by writers like Wiesel and Ka-tzetnik who depicted the Holocaust experience from within. The task is to shatter all accepted norms and values so as to vivify to the reader the experience of *l'univers concentrationnaire*. The terrifying effect of Bartov's use lies in the transformation of the 'other planet' experience into post-Holocaust reality.

Thus, Bartov employs this major Jewish problem – Jewish identity – as exemplifying the post-Holocaust situation. Although the actual event of the catastrophe in Europe is not focused on, its aftermath is affecting everyone. Elisha's reaction to this episode reflects the author's attitude, as he says "only over the years did that identification parade become what is now a searing shame within me." He even feels it physically as a "shame burning beneath my skin"; its memory lasting for years (p. 128).

Vengeance

The question of Jewish identity is related in the novel to the question of vengeance. While the expressed mission of the Jewish Brigade was one of rescue, another aspect of it was to fight the Germans. Having been too late for that, there is a substitute urge for vengeance. As portrayed by Bartov, the two aspects of the mission conflict with, if not contradict, each other. Apart from this apparent dilemma, there is the deep-rooted question of the nature of the desired vengeance.

A great deal of emphasis is placed by Bartov on this question of vengeance. Various personages are made to express different, and opposing, views as to whether the Jewish Brigade should devote itself after the war to rescuing the remaining Jews or to avenging the dead. In addition to the two opposing views, that of rescue and that of vengeance, Bartov raises another one, which prevails. It is the notion that inherently Jews must exhibit their weakness and impotence by not being able to act like Russians or any other people in a war situation. Associated with their inability to act as a result of historical processes that affected them is the Jewish moral code.

Portraying the apparent impotence to act in vengeance is so dominant in the novel that it must lead to some search for the reason why the Jewish soldiers could not act in vengeance. While Bartov does not address himself directly to this question, the explanations are inscribed within the novel and within its characters. On the one hand, the lack of a zealous adherence to Judaism inhibits one from resorting to the biblical version of revenge. On the other hand, it is another version of Judaism, diaspora Judaism, rather vague in its essence, that is being proposed as having its impact on Elisha; it is some sort of Jewish morality as being preached and practiced throughout two thousand years of mostly passive (in a political sense) Jewish existence.

One may detect some residue of the tension that existed in Hebrew literature earlier in the twentieth century between the adherents to a Dionysian type of early Hebrew civilization (advocated by such writers as Micha Yoseph Berdichevsky and Shaul Tschernichovsky) and its opposing form of cerebral and moralistic Judaism (of which Ahad Ha'am – Asher Ginsberg – and Hayim Nahman Bialik were the spokesmen).

Yet there is also the painful notion of the meaninglessness of any vengeance in comparison with the atrocities. This author believes that Bartov endeavors to promulgate this idea. He exemplifies this notion in a symbolic act of vengeance as the Palestinian Jewish soldiers are facing, for the first time, the defeated German army. The act, full of frustration, is of import: they throw "a cheap facsimile [statuette] of Moses" (p. 63) at the war prisoners. That is indeed a mockery of vengeance. This act signifies their discarding the biblical, Mosaic vengefulness for its cheap imitation.

Elisha realizes the meaninglessness of this type of revenge as he is confronted with an attempt of some of his comrades to rape two German women. He rescues the two women as he threatens to shoot his friends, firing his only shot on this occasion.

It is an act of frustration and desperation. It crystallizes the terrible predicament of these Jewish soldiers: having a desire and need to avenge the atrocities yet being unable to do so.

By creating a Holocaust-related reality of the post-war period, it is expected that an author should be evaluated not only by his narrative art, his craftsmanship in characterization and composition of the story, or by his style, but also by his unique conceptualization of the Holocaust. It is not a direct message about the Holocaust per se as presented by a given author; it is rather an all-engulfing, powerful concept that presents the truth of the event as perceived uniquely by the artist and emanating from his work.

In his novel Bartov highlights a major concept which is integrated within the fundamental structure and inner texture and fabric of the story. It is referred to in those features of detachment, belatedness, late encounters, and self-revelation which were discussed above. The author accentuates the inability of the outsider to fathom the Holocaust, its consequences, and its historic meaning. To the outsider, the Holocaust is unbearable and its conceptualization is unattainable in the abstract. It appears to defy all known human experience. Thus the outsider expects, as did the Palestinian soldiers, to witness a European reality which will be synonymous with the image he has formed of the Holocaust. That image is essentially a concretization of the abstract.

Europe Is Not Covered with Blood

Somehow, the outsider expects, nay yearns, to see Europe "covered with blood" (p. 80) at the end of the war. This image may be regarded as metaphoric, having its roots in the Bible (and elsewhere). Covering the blood of a person (with earth) or exposing one's blood will generally indicate an attempt to cover up or reveal, respectively, one's responsibility or guilt for the death of that person. Three biblical examples may suffice to explain the original use of the biblical idiom. Judah, trying to save Joseph, says to his brothers: "What do we gain by killing our brother and covering up [*Vechisinu*, Hebrew meaning "cover"] his blood" (*Genesis* 37:26). Job protests his unjust punishment (metaphoric death or bloodshed), saying: "Earth, do not cover my blood" (*Job* 16:18). And finally, upon God's mission of retribution, the prophet Isaiah exclaims: "The Lord shall come forth from His place to punish the dwellers of the earth for their iniquity; and the earth shall disclose its bloodshed, and shall no longer conceal its slain" (*Isaiah* 26:21).

In all these examples the Hebrew verb *KiSaH* or its antonym *GiLaH* are associated with blood. The third verse exemplifies the connection between retribution and the earth's disclosure of the blood concealed in it.

While Bartov does not explicitly use the biblical idiom, he infers it in his selection of words in Hebrew (*"Eiropah mechusah dam"*),[11] thus evoking the original biblical image. It is here as elsewhere in the post-Holocaust reality of the novel that biblical concepts are proven incongruous to the modern setting. The personal or national subconscious desire to resort to archetypal biblical acts is not even manifested in the conscious, overt use of language, let alone adherence to original biblical concepts. Further discussion on this point will follow.

Expecting to witness Europe covered with blood, the outsider realizes much to his shock that "here all was a pastoral" (p. 80). A landscape that does not reflect the atrocities of the war welcomes the Jewish soldiers in Europe, and it overwhelms them in its beauty and its serenity. Bartov delineates this aspect of reality as a devastating force that inhibits the avengers from fulfilling the mission they undertook upon themselves. It is another discovery that enhances the movement of the novel toward the culmination of its internal truth.

More importantly, another aspect of uncovering what is behind a facade is related not to landscape but to people. Much to his horror, the first-person narrator discovers that the faces of German collaborators or sympathizers, and even of Nazis, "were no different than faces anywhere in the world; no matter how hard we tried we could not make out the features of the devil's henchmen in those townspeople" (p. 80).

There is an attempt to get to the roots of the Holocaust phenomenon; there is an attempt to unfold the hidden truth which lies behind the facade. It is not an easy task, as we have seen. Europe is not covered with blood as they thought and wished it to be; and the face of German collaborators and Nazi sympathizers look quite normal to the naked eye. This must have been a shocking revelation for the Jewish soldiers. Elisha is made to experience a more traumatic discovery as he looks at a book with the *Führer's* picture in it. The narrator reports of his reactions: "He [Hitler] seemed just like the

---

11. *Pitz'ei Bagrut*, p. 76 [Hebrew].

rest of the book – very civil [...] Already he, too, seemed human to me [...] there was no 'murder in the eyes.'" The narrator painfully concludes: "The truth did not float like oil on water" (p. 68). It appears that the outsiders may have expected the proverbial biblical enactment of "Truth springs up from the earth" (*Psalms* 85:12), a concept related to that of earth disclosing its blood. However, as biblical vengefulness is foreign to modern-day, secular reality, in the post-Holocaust context so is biblical truth.

The post-Holocaust realization that on the surface everything looked the same as in pre-Holocaust is attested here as in other creative and documentary writings on the Holocaust. As discussed in a previous chapter, Ka-tzetnik capitalized on this concept in his *Star Eternal*. His angle, of course, was that of a survivor, which makes the 'business as usual' type of attitude hard to accept. Bartov is struggling with outsiders' attitudes, and he attempts to give these attitudes a literary reality of their own. Obviously, Bartov addresses himself to the weakness of the outsider. It stems from the detached, noncommittal stand which an outsider such as Elisha appears to have taken. It also stems from his attitude toward diaspora Jews. Bartov portrays his protagonist as being unable to relate to his fellow Jews, those survivors of the Holocaust.

Psychological problems of guilt, as well as practical limitations to come to the rescue of individual survivors and groups of survivors, inhibit the lofty mission of the Jewish Brigade. A messianic, euphoric feeling on the part of a group of Hungarian Jewish survivors is thus shattered, as reality overshadows the religious dreams and hopes replaced by mundane facts of life (p. 93). The Brigade was ill-prepared for the mission, as indeed the paradigmatic events that took place throughout the novel clearly show. It is not only the limitation of the soldiers but also the unpreparedness of the survivors. Esther, surviving by using false *Volksdeutsche* papers, is unwilling to give up her security, and prefers her current status to the one offered by the Palestinian Jews (p. 95). Bartov describes the mutual unpreparedness of both rescuers and survivors, and thus the great tragedy of the post-Holocaust effects on the Jewish people. It is the inability to adjust to the new reality that overcame the survivors, a motif emphasized in Holocaust literature. It is also the inability of the redeemers to transmit the message loud and clear to the survivors.

It is further the inability of the outsiders to identify with the fate of the survivors and perhaps to understand fully the horrors of the catastrophe. They are forever to remain as outsiders because deep in their hearts they wish it. Elisha's attitude toward his relative Krochmal, a former inmate who managed to survive by working in the crematorium, is one of "revulsion" (p. 161), and an ambiguous shame (p. 162). It is through an encounter such as this that Bartov recreates the post-Holocaust reality. The closeness of Elisha to Krochmal through their family ties does bring to bear a more acute relationship between the two. Elisha's apparently critical attitude toward the survivor reflects his subconscious realization of the nature of his own survival. While Elisha epitomizes the volunteer who could not stand the attitude of passivity in Palestine during the war, he nevertheless represents the Jews and the world *in toto* whose survival may be said to be comparable to that of Krochmal.

"We Are All Survivors"

If we accept the notion that we are all survivors, as asserted by Steiner,[12] we must also accept the tragic consequence that in the post-Holocaust reality we are all also Krochmals. The subtlety of Elisha's guilt would testify to this effect.

Unlike the writings of Wiesel and Ka-tzetnik on the Holocaust experience and Gouri's and Amichai's on the post-Holocaust consequences (see the respective chapters), Bartov's style is less intense, less condensed, and less poetic. As will be discussed in the following chapters, Gouri and Amichai, being both poets and prose writers, their poetic inclinations are outstanding even in their prose. Bartov is more of a prose writer. His Hebrew style is standard, employed to represent authentically the experience of the Palestinian Jews through their language of expression. Nothing in his style makes his writing in any inherent way related to the Holocaust experience, as indeed is the case with some of the other writers named above.

However, as pointed out before, use of the language of the Bible, namely Hebrew, cannot but evoke at times images from the Bible. References are made to a contemporary analogy of the biblical flood upon arriving in Germany close to the end of their cavalcade ("We lifted the flap of our tent, like Noah on Ararat," p. 210). However, these images are rather weak as they are not enhanced to become intrinsic, dominant motifs in the novel. Their presentation is incidental while still drawing on the biblical story of the flood and Noah.

A similar reference in the end barely alludes to the overturning of Sodom and Gomorrah ("My thoughts turned to pillars of salt," p. 246). The use of the cheap imitation of the figure of Moses, cited earlier, is perhaps more meaningful. A reference to the biblical story of Joseph and Potiphar's wife (p. 202) contributes little to the story. Yet a related reference, in that immediate context, to Jonathan's tasting of the honey (p. 202) is more meaningful. An attempt to intensify the biblical expression "worm of Jacob" (p. 157, *Isaiah* 41:14) as related to the experience of the brigade's

---

12. George Steiner, *Language and Silence* (New York, 1967), p. 145.

convoy is not too successful, as it lacks the emotional message of the biblical text.

One should then conclude that biblical language and biblical images do not constitute a significant part of Bartov's art as they are not central to his protagonists' milieu but serve as an echo to Elisha's upbringing. More essential to the overall message of the novel are some references from the New Testament or the Hebrew prayer book.

Using references to events in Jewish history is more convincing; however, this, too, appears to be a minor phenomenon in Bartov's writing. Before the scene of the attempted rape of the two German women as an act of vengeance, Elisha is made to dream of a pogrom in which he is persecuted among other Jews (pp. 227–228). His subconscious association with his Jewish past helps explain the nature of his act against the Jewish soldiers' attempt to rape the women.

Elisha's discovery of himself is now complete. He still wishes to flee (p. 233) as before, except that now Elisha is aware of his problem, having faced it, and he has arrived at a decision: "I would [...] do anything to escape that continent where I could not live either with our dead or with their living" (p. 233).

Aware of his persistent weakness, Elisha is nevertheless thankful for it, uttering in the end: "*Thank God I did not destroy myself in Germany, thank God that was beyond me. I am what I am*" (p. 246). By evoking the biblical expression of God referring to his own name as "*Eheyeh asher eheyeh* [I am who I am]" (*Exodus* 3:14), Bartov seems to integrate the sacred identity of the divine with his own secular, modern concept of Elisha's identity. Elisha is portrayed as he is, forever bound to his heritage. He realizes that in spite of everything, he must be Jewish. As expressed so eloquently by another Hebrew writer, Aharon Appelfeld, a survivor: "'*Al korhacha yehudi atah*" (Against your will, you are Jewish)....[13]

---

13. In an article "Ha'eimah Vehahit'hayvut" [Horror and Commitment] published in *Ma'ariv* Literary Supplement, August 8, 1975, and in *Masot Beguf Rishon* [Essay in First Person] (Jerusalem, 1979), p. 24 [Hebrew].

Chapter 7
Hayim Gouri: Concept of Post-Holocaust Reality in *The Chocolate Deal*

The distance of the Israeli authors of the 1948 generation from the experience of the Shoah itself and consequently from addressing it in a direct way in their writing is a known and understood phenomenon. With the exception of Aharon Appelfeld who is a survivor, most contemporary Israeli writers dealt with the Holocaust as by-standers, writing about it after the event itself. As discussed in the chapter on *Badenheim 1939*, Appelfeld employs unique perspectives and metaphors in dealing with topics related to the Holocaust but rarely describes the realistic aspects of the Shoah, the death and suffering, which he apparently prefers not to address directly.

Thus, post-Holocaust Israeli writers examine the aftermath of the Holocaust from the outside, watching its impact on the survivors and probing its existential significance to the post-Holocaust Jew as well as to all sensitive people in general.

Some writers chose to recreate the post-Holocaust reality as a realistic meeting or as an encounter with survivors in Europe or in Israel, while others chose poetic forms, rich in intensity in language and structure, and based on non-realistic, symbolic foundations. This is what writers such as Hayim Gouri did in his book *The Chocolate Deal*, which is the subject of this chapter, and as Yehuda Amichai did in his *Not of This Time, Not of This Place*, to be discussed in the next chapter.[1] Initially, Gouri published *The Chocolate Deal* in Hebrew in 1965.[2]

---

1.   Haim Gouri, *The Chocolate Deal*, trans. by Seymour Simckes (New York: Holt, Rinehart and Winston, 1968); another edition by Wayne State University Press, with an introduction by Geoffrey Hartman, was published in Detroit in 1999. Both editions have the same pagination.
2.   Hayim Gouri, *Iskat Hashokolad* [The Chocolate Deal] (Tel Aviv, 1965).

Gouri's and Amichai's writings are of special interest because both of them are poets writing in prose which is essentially poetic. Studying their works may enrich our sensitivities and understanding of the Holocaust as perceived and conceived by great literary artists.

Gouri's novel depicts the destroyed lives of two survivors of the Holocaust: Rubi – Reuben Krauss, and Mordi – Mordecai Neuberg, in a German city immediately after the war. The two survivors are trying to reconstruct their lives. While the only solution for Mordi is death, Rubi is characterized as a man of action and of great vision and plans. Reflecting the precarious moral predilection of people after the war, Gouri delineates Rubi as having no scruples, benefitting from the war by whatever means possible, whether legitimate or not. Rubi envisions a scheme in which he will ask Dr. Karl Hoffman, whose daughter he presumably rescued from a burning building, to reward him by partaking in a plot of the chocolate deal. The doctor is to issue a false medical report that the chocolate supplied by the military is tainted with a tranquilizing matter intended to "pacify bold lonely men on duty" (p. 120). Consequently the price of the chocolate will go down and Rubi and the doctor will buy a large quantity at a low price. The scheme is that afterwards the doctor will rescind the report as erroneous, the price of chocolate will go up, and that will give both of them hefty profits (p. 124).

Presentation of 'Unreal' Reality

While the story has an external plot, Gouri is more interested in the protagonists' inner lives. He externalizes their lives on the surface by their actions and words. Yet, these actions and words within the context of the novel are related to overall national issues, such as whether or not to accept reparations from Germany. This was a major ethical dilemma in the 1950s and 1960s, which is implied through the chocolate deal.

Various components of the novel do not carry a unified and clear treatment. They include the characterization, depiction of reality, description of background and surroundings, transition of time, and the development of plot. Gouri prefers to present the post-Holocaust reality in a peculiar way that annuls and obliterates the regular rules of the known and familiar reality. Instead, he creates a different set of rules for reality and its depiction. In so doing he is trying to give an authentic artistic expression to the phenomenon of the post-Holocaust condition of the survivors.

Studying Gouri's literary art, as with other writers discussed in this book, may contribute to our understanding of the unique nature of literature of the Holocaust.

Crossroads of Past and Present

The exposition of *The Chocolate Deal* is case in point. At the outset, the novel looks realistic, but the depiction is intensified beyond mere description as the narrator evokes meaningful images from the past, reminiscent of the Holocaust. Gouri has purposefully selected events and occurrences in order to apprise the reader about the unique impact that the Shoah has had on the lives of survivors after the war. Thus, the first lines in the opening of the novel describe in the present tense the arrival of the train which takes place after the war. Yet, it is worded in such a way that it transposes the protagonist who turned out to be a survivor back to the experience of the Holocaust: "...at last the train is here. Is here at last" (p. 1). As one of the main instruments associated with the Holocaust, the train transporting people to their death, is such an intrinsic part of the Holocaust that its image evokes a direct reference to the Shoah. In effect, the train became a symbol of the Shoah, and it appears in several stories discussed so far.

The figure of the narrator, whose role is not clear at first, begins to echo past events, creating analogies that relate the story's present to the past. Concurrently, the reader notices also the peculiar presence of the narrator who is in effect witnessing the events. As the train comes close, the narrator comments with an 'editorial' voice, "As before. As always" (p. 1). This interjection by the narrator contributes another dimension of time into the story which relates past and present and does not let the past fade away into oblivion.

It is there that the two friends, Rubi and Mordi, meet. Their meeting, taking place in the crossroad of past and present, is imbued with gloomy signs and symbols. Gouri intensifies the described reality which confronts the two protagonists, as well as the reader, with concreteness that is borrowed from other times and other places. He creates this foreboding atmosphere by purposefully citing selected names, such as a soup kitchen in "Bat Alley" not too far from "the statue *The Black Plague*" (p. 6). The soup is reminiscent of the survivors' experiences in the death camps. Sounds, too, are made to remind the two survivors of yesteryear; they hear some trumpets, which, it is told, are a "prelude to the marvelous victory anthem." The narrator then adds a comment: "The holy touch of dread" (p. 8), evoking an editorial statement as though it was emanating from the two silently vocal survivors.

Gouri paints the scenery with dark colors, especially black. Aside from the Black Plague, cited above (p. 6), the skies are given the color black as the "lamplights don't penetrate the dull grayness" (p. 7). Rubi "extinguishes his cigarette in [the cold soup] and the blackened butt floats on the thick cold dough" (p. 8).

Not only is the soup reminiscent of the past, but there is a continuous air of doom and gloom, a sense of desperation, which fills the opening chapter. These foreboding symbols and bleak colors cast their dark shadows throughout the novel and set its overall tone.

Shifting Points of View

As the novel unfolds, the point-of-view shifts from Rubi to Mordi, and from each of them to an unknown ubiquitous narrator who follows them and makes continuous comments on their activities. His omnipresence and omniscience are a unique feature of the novel.

It has been already noted that in the opening scene the narrator has made the comment, "As always. As before" (p. 1), adding another dimension of time to the story, which takes place in the present. Right there and then, as the narrator tells of the tall man descending from the train, the reader hears another comment in the form of rhetorical questions, "Is he waiting for someone? Does he have time to spare?" (p. 1).

The interjection in the form of a general observation by an omniscient narrator continues: "As a rule, names don't show on faces [...]. For him, therefore it's possible to carry around a remnant of pride" (pp. 1–2). It is "inconceivable," it is told, that he may have some other clothes with him; but immediately afterwards the narrator arouses the curiosity of the reader with more rhetorical questions: "What's hidden in that small suitcase? What could be hidden there?" (p. 2).

The protagonist, the narrator reports, pulls out a pack of cheap cigarettes, and the narrator's comment comes immediately "– what else?" (p. 2). And then, a rhetorical question, "How long is a man like him permitted to stand around, altogether unoccupied, without arousing wonder or suspicion?" (p. 2).

Consequently, the narrator interjects comments on another level of perception: "*Most likely* he's looking for someone. *Perhaps* the man who didn't wait for him on the platform?"; "...the man *must* find this business interesting. Look. Right now, *for example*, he sits on the stone bench" (p. 3). As the two meet, the narrator tells that they form a twisted sculpture "entitled, *perhaps*, 'The Reunion'" (p. 4). And then he comments, "It's *unfortunate*, but they do not even notice..." (p. 7; italics added).

An Open-Ended Story; a Possible Story

The narrator seems to be standing on the sideline and making comments, asking leading questions whose answers are to be found later on in the novel. The purpose of the questions is to arouse the reader's curiosity in an attempt to explore this enigmatic figure. Thus, the narrator endeavors to involve the reader as a by-stander in the reality and in the issues of the novel. The questions also indicate that the narrator himself is in effect an involved narrator. He has some other characteristics that affect his role in the novel. He is a narrator-editor who is making comments and is offering interpretations, and he has something to say about the protagonists and their values.

Hayim Gouri created a unique atmosphere in his novel by employing loaded terms such as *"Most likely," "Perhaps," "for example,"* which were cited before. These words form the inner thrust of the novel not as a story of events that occurred in the past but as a 'possibility,' a likelihood of events that may or may not have happened. Whether 'real' or imagined, apparently the narrator has no control over the protagonists and their actions, and ostensibly does not know how things will develop in the story. The narrator leads the reader, so to speak, to a possible reality, an open reality, as if it were not a story that took place already, a closed story, which has a beginning and an end, but as an open-ended story.

In his unique artistic way Gouri created a Holocaust-related story that is not bound by the accepted rules of conventional reality, or, for that matter, conventional fiction. He sets up this conceptual literary infra-structure in the novel's format in order to highlight the great tragedy of the Shoah and its aftermath. This is his unique perception of the Holocaust as affecting people's lives in the post-war years. It intends especially to emphasize the fate of the survivors for whom the Holocaust experience was not over in 1945. The Shoah twisted the existence, values, and life-patterns of millions of people, but the fate of those Jews who survived it is worse because their lives have been distorted forever.

The post-war reality, as presented in Gouri's novel, reflects some of the unreal, distorted, and dreadful aspects of the Holocaust in their effects on the survivors. Established frameworks and conventions of time and place are portrayed as totally twisted; past and present are intertwined and both touch some uncertain future, which is also foggy and ambiguous, and may even be only a possibility. Reality and imagination are interwoven; abrupt transitions stir the protagonists and the reader as they move from one plane to another, from one sphere to another. Their sum total is existential chaos which lacks any familiar criteria for measurement and assessment. Similar techniques appear in modern novels intended to depict disorientation and alienation, but their use here for depicting the post-Holocaust reality transcends the literary goals, intensifying the unique perception of the Shoah and its implication for humanity.

The Inner Monologue

To facilitate his unique depiction of post-Holocaust reality, Gouri uses the technique of the inner monologue – where the protagonist speaks to himself in first person – in his narrative for various purposes. At times, the shift from third person to an inner monologue seems to be abrupt. For example, "It seems to him, it just seems to him that he has an address, says Rubi in his heart..." This point of view shifts in the next sentence to an inner monologue that is not distinguished in the text by quotation marks (which are supplied here): "The Salomons will recognize me" (p. 12). Actually, the original Hebrew has the last sentence as an inner monologue in third person, while the English reverted to first person. In so doing, Gouri creates an obscure view of a questionable reality, reflecting the confused states of the individual described.

The arbitrary transition from third-person narrative to first-person voice causes an air of ambiguity. In the following sentence, the narrator describes Mordi examining his friend Rubi in third person: "Now he examines the man standing opposite him..." (p. 4) And immediately in the next paragraph there is an abrupt shift to an inner monologue: "And so it *is* him. Apparently it's him. After all" (p. 5). It is followed by an inner monologue in first person without quotation marks (which are given here), as if it were a continuation of the narrative: "Even so, passed here by accident. I came over to buy cigarettes..." (p. 5).

At times Gouri uses the inner monologue to facilitate a transition from the events as they are apparently taking place in the present to flashback scenes from the past.

The switches from the inner monologue leading to the flashbacks vary and they are not unified. For example, the narrator presents Rubi's inner monologue: "He never wasted his time [...] he always had time left over for 'What did you learn today?' or a look of infinite tenderness" (p. 13).

Then, immediately afterwards, the text shifts to an event that took place in the past but is related to the inner monologue: "One day the teacher said to Father, 'Mr. Krauss, your son is a genius in mathematics'" (p. 13).

On other occasions there is a shift from the inner monologue to the narrative. For example: the inner monologue, "I'll recognize the place..." shifts immediately afterwards in the next paragraph to the narrative in third person: "Uncle Salomon didn't handle small-fry criminal cases..." (p. 14). This technique, too, creates some tension between the various points of view, which results in a vague view of reality as presented in the novel.

Distortion of Time

This use of the inner monologue is related also to another central technique used by Gouri – the distortion of time. A scene that opens in the present tense switches without any warning to the future tense: "'Have a cigarette,' says Mordi. Come at once, they'll answer, we're waiting for you, Rubi, on pins and needles" (p. 15). Rubi appears to imagine what may happen in the future. Yet several sentences later, which use future tense, the narrative shifts to the present, as if things are occurring right there and then. Thus, through the inner monologue, Gouri is able to combine imagination and reality into one unified, yet vague, structure whose rules attempt to emulate those that were established in the Holocaust reality from which the survivors cannot escape.

Eliminating the separate partitions between the real and the imagined is done through inserting a dialogue taking place in the present into the imagined dialogue: "'That's not the way it's done,'" says Mordi. 'Why not?' 'It's not done.' Following this real dialogue, the next sentence is an imagined dialogue which cites the speakers as if in a script of a play: "Rubi: 'Gerti, tell Uncle Salomon I'm here. Waiting. Downstairs'" (p. 24). It is an imagined statement by Rubi. The real dialogue between Rubi and Mordi is inserted into the imagined dialogue between Rubi and Gerti. The English translation reproduced these dialogues line by line, whereas the Hebrew has them set continuously without any paragraph break. Also, the English introduced the speaker with colons: "Rubi:" whereas the Hebrew does not cite the speakers, which makes the sentence flow more smoothly, yet read more confusing.

These statements are totally imagined, yet they continue the real dialogue without any mark of change. And following these imagined dialogues, the novel resorts to continue the real dialogue that was interrupted before: "'Why isn't it done?' 'I'm just advising you'" (p. 24).

The key to Gouri's unique handling of the novel's structure is provided in the novel itself in one of Rubi's inner monologues: "Without doubt, a chain of simultaneous activities is somewhat marvelous; you're washing yourself and at the same time the coffee warms up for you and at the same time the telephone rings" (p. 25). Compressing the elements of time to their 'telescopic' concept of concurrency deviates from the conventional dimensions of time and suggests the survivors' distorted reality. This confused reality brings the survivors back to the other 'planet' which has different elements of time and existence, where horror, disorientation, and unpredictable events reign supreme. While this portrayal of reality is not identical to that of the Holocaust, it does attempt to recreate an analogous situation through literary means.

The Possible Terrible Fire and Its Significance

The author's creative perception of the Shoah is best illustrated by the central event described in the novel. It is a "terrible fire" that broke out in a building from which Rubi rescues a blond German girl (pp. 26–29). All of Gouri's literary techniques which were cited above are found in this chapter. The very beginning of the fire story refers to it as "the possibility of that terrible fire" (p. 26). This use of words throws in that element of uncertainty as to whether it really occurred or it is part of the protagonist's imagination. The story is prefaced with a direct dialogue which fuses into an inner monologue. It is imbued with historical and biblical allusions which enhance the fire to a very meaningful cataclysmic event. It is a "frightful fire which often breaks out...," Rubi comments in his inner monologue, and summarizes it by the biblical reference to "Sodom and Gomorrah" (p. 26), extending the event beyond its immediate scope. The rescue activities and the sirens of the fire trucks, "that terrifying rushing wail, reminder of salvation that has often come too late" carry a message with a concluding comment from another time and another place. "The dramas enacted there," it is told in that inner monologue, "recall the very first catastrophe, Primordial Chaos" (p. 26). The conflagration is definitely extended beyond a mere building fire. In addition, it appears as though the firefighters in their haste used oil instead of water and caused the flames to rise (p. 27), which adds an element of irony, perhaps incredibility, to the event as described.

Additional references to "Hell" and "burning Rome" in the description of the flames contribute to the sense of a major event. Also, there are Rubi's leading questions which add to the 'mystery' yet may provide some clues to its solution:

Who created [...] a vision so absurd, so gorgeous? For what purpose? What frenzied poet turned his sick imagination or his blind desire for revenge into fact? What does he, Rubi, have to do with all this? Why did the fire seize this respectable apartment house, and who's the arsonist? (p. 27).

All of those references and loaded questions, at times rhetorical questions, do imply a fire which is more than an ordinary fire. It is an event that transcends itself and is written with such intensity and planted clues as to achieve a level of symbolism.

The Survivor Rescues the Blond German Girl

Does this event really constitute the main thrust of the novel?

The continuation of the story proves otherwise; it invalidates any notion that this event is a symbol by reducing it from its context of historical allusions to a mundane setting. It contains a depiction of actions and an exchange of practical dialogues, which takes place in the present. No longer is it a "possibility of that terrible fire."

At this point Rubi's act of rescuing the girl is described in minute detail, with a shade of the melodramatic. There is excessive information and an attempt to sound matter-of-factly, perhaps to cover up the author's intention or perhaps to allude to it. Now told in the present tense, Rubi heroically climbs up the ladder until he is lost in the dark cloud. The narrator continues to insert in his description some more phrases loaded with biblical and religious images: "As if on the merit of Mishael and Azariah," naming the two Israelites thrown into the furnace together with Daniel because they adhered to their Jewish heritage. Rubi is described as "a burning angel" (p. 28). He goes into the fire and rescues the girl.

Does Gouri want to allude to what one critic, Moshe Gil, called "the great fire that consumed the house of Israel in Europe"?[3] Are the various allusions referring to a representation of the Shoah?

The continuation of the story leads to another interpretation. It is noticeable in the description of the aftermath of the fire and rescue as it unfolds in the dialogue between the father, Dr. Hoffman, and Rubi. "'How can I thank you? How can I repay you?'" asks the grateful father. "'I did my duty,' says he, Rubi, and breaks the hearts of those gathered around...'" (p. 29).

One notices an ironic reversal of roles: ostensibly, now the Jew is the rescuer and the German is the rescued 'victim.' Being thanked for his deeds, the Jew gives an answer reminiscent of similar answers in reversal of roles where the perpetrators of the crimes justified their acts by saying, "I did my duty." This imagined dialogue is followed with the statement of people's exaggerated reaction as Rubi 'breaks their hearts.'

This dialogue between the two may allude to possible development in the novel as indeed Dr. Hoffman is called to reward Rubi for his deed.... The exchange between the two ends with a summary description which has the tone of exaggeration:

> Truly, there's nothing, not even salt in the eyes, that arouses so much genuine feeling as the sight of heroism, that self-sacrifice, body and soul, which the heroes themselves consider a matter of course – those heroes who clam up before thank-yous and hurrahs (p. 29).

This tone of exaggeration that reaches the realm of satire tends to contradict the ostensible authenticity and the seemingly straight-forward reporting of this act of heroism and rescue.

---

3. Moshe Gil, in a review article on "Iskat Hashokolad" [*The Chocolate Deal*], in *Moznayim*, 20 (43, December 1965–May 1965), p. 381 [Hebrew].

The interplay of tones and depictions gets another twist as the narrator resorts to a full newspaper's report of the event, including "giant headlines and pictures" in the style of news reporting:

'GIRL OF TEN RESCUED
FROM BURNING HOUSE.
A RARE DISPLAY OF COURAGE.'

'Reuben (Rubi) Krauss, a refugee without citizenship status and without work, who lives with his friend in a little cellar [...] yesterday displayed an unusual daring by climbing a fireman's ladder up to the seventh floor of a burning house and rescuing the only daughter of Dr. Karl Hoffman' (p. 30).

Again, it is an attempt to present the event objectively and authentically for no one can dispute a newspaper's report. However, the report also ends with a loaded statement: "'Charlotte Hoffman is in perfect condition'" (p. 30).

Atonement, Consciousness, and Reparations

The meaning of Rubi's act of rescuing the German girl in the context of the Holocaust is provided toward the end of the novel as Rubi carries on an imagined conversation with Dr. Hoffman (about the chocolate deal) and cites Mordi's (imagined?) reaction to the act of rescuing the German girl.

As a survivor, Mordi preferred death over acquiescing to moral rehabilitation of the guilty perpetrators of the Holocaust. As cited by Rubi, Mordi considered his act "a kind of betrayal" (p. 128), sort of a "false play," which he defined as follows: when "you atone, in one moment, for the long crime against the many" (p. 129). Accordingly, Mordi was of the opinion that Rubi should have "'let [Hoffman's] daughter burn,'" and since he did not let her die, "the cry of the other girls is heard." Dr. Hoffman, in this imaginary conversation, asks, "'What others?'" And Rubi retorts: "'All those in whose behalf nobody climbed up to the seventh floor'" (p. 129).

Through the distortion of cause and effect and a reversal of roles in the post-Holocaust reality, Hayim Gouri tells a story of the Jew who saves Charlotte, a blond-haired representation of the German people, from "hellish fire of conscience pangs and the flames of shame and infamy," as stated by Moshe Gil, in his above cited article.[4]

For this reason, and for saving the consciousness of the German people, Rubi demands something in return, exemplified in the story by the chocolate deal, from which he wants to benefit. The story's chocolate deal and the monetary rewards expected from it allude to the reparations from Germany which occupied the public debate in the 1950s in Israel and

---

4. *Ibid.*

abroad. It created a bitter controversy between those who objected to accepting any compensation whatsoever from post-war Germany, and those who would accept German's reparations but would not forgive nor forget Nazi atrocities perpetrated against the Jewish people and others.

Rubi is portrayed as the archetype of the Jewish survivor who is willing to reconcile calamities of the past for the possible rewards of the present. His willingness to resolve the ethical and conscience problem of accepting reparations from Germany is not portrayed by Gouri only as criticism and accusation against accepting reparations. More importantly, Gouri depicts the human condition of the Jewish individual in the post-Holocaust era and the paradoxes that he has to cope with because of his decision to go on living regardless of the past. The past, for him, is suppressed, while subconsciously affecting him, and the present is apparently a possibility for the future.

Rubi's relationship with Gerti, the German girl, places the notion of forgetfulness as a function of eros – a recurring theme in Holocaust literature, especially in Amichai's novel *Not of This Time, Not of This Place*, to which a chapter is devoted later.

Mordi's Quest for Another Place

Mordi, on the other hand, is the hesitating, agonizing type who "knew where he came from, and where he was," but does not know where to go (p. 10) in his attempt to grasp the meaning of the Shoah. In Mordi's inner monologue Gouri exposes some insights about him. Mordi wishes, for the time being, "...to move and think and change. We'll go and adjust ourselves accordingly." He is willing to "go from here to another land, we'll go and try it out. Meanwhile we can look for an address." Mordi is desirous to make changes: "... We can make a new start in a new place. We'll get other clothes. Get other names" (p. 18). In this characterization of Mordi, Gouri raises the question of the survivor's identity and his sense of belonging, or lack thereof, in the aftermath of the Shoah.

While on a quest for his new place and role, Mordi's solution is death (p. 96) – the complete surrender to the fate of the victims of the Holocaust and finally joining them.

Gouri expresses his awareness of the tantalizing dilemma which confronts survivors and sensitive people concerning the post-Holocaust issue of forgetting, perhaps forgiving, in a monologue with a poetic touch:

Slowly, slowly the roads turn to meet. Time passes; that quack doctor gives a drug of forgetfulness to the hurt to quiet them and push them on further. It sends the lost to sleep the sleep that lasts and lasts till doomsday. An abyss opens between remembering and remembered, and that's where the rivers rush, that's where the year's seasons are, and that's where dark gray snow-covered cities are – cities, marble and gold from the sun. Kindled violet. And that's where the right of the wanderers is to defy silence, to dream, and go on, (p. 83).

Is it Rubi's way "to defy silence [...] and [to] go on," or Mordi's?

Rubi, who is going on with some vision, or perhaps a dream, of a possibility in the future, finds himself, at the end, near Mordi's grave. In his vision he sees himself erecting "a tombstone on Mordecai Neuberg's grave. A high granite column, lovely and dark and engraved in gold" (p. 141). In tears, he kneels "finally falling asleep" (p. 142). When he wakes up, a stranger comes toward him, asks whether he is Reuben Krauss, and tells him that Mr. Shechter is looking for him.

Mr. Shechter, it should be remembered, is a watchmaker, who knew Mordi's father before the war, and provided shelter for Mordi. Gouri characterizes Shechter as "a wise man and a man of few words" (p. 70), and as having a "sound of supervision implicit" in his voice. "It's not impossible that he's come a long way, that long ago he left all questions far behind" (p. 71). Gouri portrays him as a divine figure, a representation of divine providence.[5] He is a master of time (watchmaker) who took care of Mordi after the war. By the way, Elie Wiesel's *Night* also has a prophetic figure by the name of "Shechter" – Madame Schächter....[6]

Rubi hears the mysterious message that some providential power was calling him. Will he respond to the message?

Gouri leaves the answer as a possibility.

---

5. In the original Hebrew, the term for 'supervision' is השגחה (Hashgahah) which implies providence as well.

6. Elie Wiesel, *Night* (New York: Avon Books, 1969), p. 34.

Chapter 8
Yehuda Amichai: Fractured Soul in a Split Reality after the Holocaust in *Not of This Time, Not of This Place*

One of the prolific Israeli writers who dealt with the subject of the Holocaust is Yehuda Amichai. Known mostly as a poet, Amichai wrote prose as well and has published a collection of short stories and a long novel. In his poetry and in his prose, Amichai has displayed several motifs – some of them based on his personal life and family background – related to the Holocaust and to the destruction of European Jews during World War II.

Of special interest is his novel *Not of This Time, Not of This Place* which addresses issues related to the Shoah. It was published in Hebrew in 1963, and has been translated into English and published in 1968 in an abridged edition.[1]

The scope of Amichai's Holocaust-related writing is not as comprehensive as that of Appelfeld, whose work, as was noted previously, is totally devoted to the Shoah and its related topics such as the pre-war state of European Jewry. For Amichai, very much like other Israeli writers of the 1948 generation, the Holocaust is but one of the subjects of his interest and not necessarily the primary one. Nevertheless, his Holocaust themes are of great importance as they address issues concerning Jewish reality in the post-Holocaust period as well as attitudes toward the Shoah.

We have a great interest in Amichai because of his poetic sensitivities which are clearly noticeable also in his prose writing. Amichai's unique language quality and imagery of his poetry are also found in his prose.

---

1.   Yehuda Amichai, *Not of This Time, Not of This Place*, translated by Shlomo Katz (New York, 1968). Originally published in Hebrew as *Lo Me'achshav Lo Mikan* [Not from Now Not from Here] (Jerusalem & Tel Aviv, 1963).

Split Structure

The structure of the novel is split in two, as its plot and characters develop on two levels. This duality seems to present Amichai's concept of contemporary attitudes toward the Shoah. Accordingly, one part of the story takes place in Jerusalem while the other part occurs in Weinburg, Germany. The chapters alternate on the different levels of locality as the plot streams forward – with some flashbacks – in each consecutive chapter. Joel, the main character, is an archaeologist by profession on the Jerusalem level, who, having been born in Germany, 'digs' into the distant past of his childhood on the German level of the story.

Joel is thus split between the two aspects that form his inner life, and he must undergo the tantalizing searching and probing in order to find a remedy for his own self and for his particular circumstances. While dealing with issues related to individual characters in the story, such as Joel and his Israeli friends, the author extends his scope of vision to social and moral phenomena that confront Israeli society. Concurrently, he highlights some related aspects of German society and its Jewish population during the Holocaust and afterwards.

Exposing the protagonist's tantalizing struggle, Amichai aims to reflect the problems of the individual in their direct relationship to those of society in general. Thus, he is trying to expose the origins and trends of post-Holocaust attitudes toward the Shoah of his individual protagonists.

Exposition Depicts Post-Holocaust Reality

The opening chapter serves as the exposition, which alludes to major themes that are about to be unfolded in the novel. Employing Jewish and universal symbols, hinting at clues taken from Jewish tradition, and offering meaningful plays on words, the author attempts to re-create the Israeli reality in its alleged social and moral decadence in the post-Holocaust period.

Those were the years after the 1948 War of Independence. Following the euphoria of the apparent victory, the necessity to cope with post-war mundane realities, economic austerity, and post-Holocaust dilemmas confronted Israeli society. Amichai describes and alludes to emerging signs of deterioration and some social decay. He implies this alleged aspect of Israeli society by depicting it in a 'Roman' setting, as his protagonists engaged in a Bacchanalia. It is a group of Israelis in this Roman scenario as described by the narrator: "This was the room of the Romans. Why Romans? Because all those in this room were men who looked like Romans, like Antony and Caracalla, the stern soldier, and others" (pp. 4–5). The atmosphere is Dionysian – living the moment, experiencing sensual intoxication, and an addiction to instinctual urges. All of this is initiated by forgetting yesterday and ignoring tomorrow.

The narrator then introduces some of the novel's characters and their emblematic deeds or statements. Mina, having a 'split personality' like Joel, puts her arms around one of the pillars of the house and dramatically recites Samson's biblical phrase of doom, demise, and self destruction: "Perish my soul with the Philistines" (p. 2). Asked who the Philistines were, she says to Joel: "You, and all the rest."

The air is filled with the eucalyptus' "aroma of lust" coming from the garden which affected both of them, although they were not lovers. Amichai expands the significance of the eucalyptus by relating it to Mina's background and place in Israeli society. Like the tree, Mina was transplanted there from abroad. The original Hebrew has a play on the word *eucalyptus* which reminds Joel of 'apocalypse,' contributing to the notion of foreboding destruction.[2]

In addition, the text in the original Hebrew intensifies this notion by adding a play on words regarding the summer days and the end of days, and stating also that the roots of the eucalyptus seem to undermine the foundations of the house.[3] Thus, the narrator has depicted within the fabric of this chapter a general atmosphere of decadence and pursuit of hedonism, of a spiritual and social decline, and of some unidentified and ambiguous quest.

It is Mina who suggested that Joel fulfill his dream to go back to the town of his birth in Germany and at the same time stay in Jerusalem and get involved in a love affair. To the question what should he do first, Mina says, "You can do both at the same time" (p. 9). Thus, through Mina, Amichai has set up the basis for the structure of the novel.

Characters: Einat, Yosel, Joel and Mina

Amichai's intention to delineate the attitude of his characters toward the Holocaust is discerned in the inception of the novel. Some of the minor characters express their views openly and directly, whereas the major protagonists, mainly Joel, divulge their viewpoint as the novel continues to unfold.

Einat, an Israeli girl, represents the new generation of Israelis who is inclined to reject the *Galut* – state of exile in the Diaspora – and to suppress the Holocaust. Yosel, a survivor, is ambivalent about his past. He attempted to hide his tattooed numbers by integrating them into a mermaid design "In order to forget the past." However, he did not conceal it completely, as Joel

---

2. Amichai, *Lo Me'achshav Lo Mikan*, p. 9 [Hebrew].
3. *Ibid.*, pp. 9, 28 [Hebrew].

knew, for the opposite reason, namely, "in order to remember the past" (p. 10). Eventually, Yosel goes back to Germany (p. 201). This contradictory attitude reflects the ambiguity displayed by many Israelis and some survivors toward the Holocaust. Moreover, it exposes Amichai's own equivocation about remembering and forgetting which will be developed in the ensuing pages.

The main characters are naturally more developed in the novel. Both Joel and Mina are depicted as living on two different levels of reality. Both had been transplanted from their original birthplace overseas, like that proverbial eucalyptus. As discussed earlier, their depiction in the introductory chapter is intended to provide the background for events to come. Recording their conversations, the narrator remarks rather off-handedly that they "did not know where they belonged" (p. 2).[4]

Such a loaded statement typifies Amichai's style in presenting the dual level components of the novel. This statement is ambivalent because of the very meaning of the word *belong* (or in the original Hebrew, 'their place'). For it may be understood physically as referring to their location or spiritually, establishing their confused state of mind.

As an archaeologist, Joel undertakes to *excavate* into his own past. His name alludes to the biblical prophet Joel who is a prophet of doom. In a similar vein, the narrator reports that Joel has a feeling of demise:

Early this summer, unexpectedly, an awareness of the end descended upon him. He noted a distinct resemblance to his father, who became despondent and began to sink and died in the arms of his wife Ruth before his time. Then, suddenly, Joel began to re-examine his life [...] and in doing so his life acquired a new orientation (p. 4).

Similar themes of the resemblance between father and son and the father's death are found in Amichai's short stories and poems.[5] The resemblance to his father is a recurring motif in Amichai's writings which extends beyond the sheer physical aspect to include the spiritual as well.

Amichai's Language and Imagery

Another central motif in the novel is presented through the character of Mina. She says to Joel, "It's necessary to open a door and a window – some prophet Elijah will come in – he must come and redeem us" (p. 5).

---

4. Hebrew: "they did not know their place," *ibid.*, p. 8.

5. See Yehuda Amichai, "The Times My Father Died," in *Facing The Holocaust*, Selected Israeli Fiction, Gila Ramras-Rauch and Joseph Michman-Melkman, ed. (Philadelphia, 1985), pp. 261–272. *Cf.* his poem "Avi" [My Father] which was published with an English translation in *The Modern Hebrew Poem Itself*, Stanley Burnshaw, T. Carmi & Ezra Spicehandler, ed. (New York, 1965), p. 166.

This reference is typical of Amichai's style. His imagery and linguistic mastery draws on the vast heritage of Jewish sacred texts which serve for his intertextual references. His allusions to the sacred texts are presented with a poetic twist. At times, he secularizes the text and lowers it to its literal or mundane context. Thus, he creates some tension between the sacred and the secular, the holy and the profane, and the past and the present. In so doing, he exemplifies the very problem which confronts modern Hebrew literature and modern Hebrew language in employing the sacred texts of Scriptures and post-biblical literature in a modern setting. In a general way this is also the problem of modern Israel, facing its long tradition in the context of the modern, mostly secular, setting.

Case in point is Mina's cited statement about opening the door so that the prophet Elijah may enter. Amichai is alluding to the Passover Seder custom to open the door for Elijah and recite a prayer. This reference has a multiplicity of meanings. Firstly, in the text of the novel itself, the reference to redemption ("and redeem us") is based on the traditional belief in Judaism that Elijah's coming would precede the coming of the Messiah, and thus the final redemption of humanity at the end of days. However, there is another meaning to the citation about Elijah. Talmudic tradition refers to Elijah as one who 'solves all questions'; in the original context it refers to religious legal matters disputed by the sages. However, in the context of the novel, Mina refers to the many problems confronting the protagonists which she wishes to be solved.

More importantly perhaps is the notion of vengeance which is alluded to in opening the door for Elijah and the recitation of the prayer. This prayer recites the *Psalms* verses that call on the Almighty to cast His wrath over the heathens who had harmed the house of Israel: "Pour out your fury on the nations that do not know You, upon the kingdoms that do not invoke Your name, for they have devoured Jacob and destroyed his home" (*Psalms* 79:6). This prayer evokes the notion of vengeance, which is a central theme in the novel.

Amichai's poetical vocabulary and system of allusions are based on the dual meaning of the text and its intertextuality; but their interpretation extends beyond the hermeneutics within the parameters of the current text. His allusions are in effect part and parcel of the author's *Weltanschauung*, which purports to establish an existential and philosophic stand through the medium of language.

An excellent example to illustrate Amichai's sophisticated use of language and imagery is found in his description of Joel's arrival by train in Weinburg:

All at once the station was abandoned by the trains. This seldom happens. The trains had left on their way and the loudspeaker fell silent, for it had nothing more to announce. All the 'rams' horns' which are usually sounded fell silent, for in stations every day is a day of decision (p. 58).

The loudspeaker's silence, which is quite common in a regular setting of a train station, is given a more meaningful context, as the verb 'to announce,' which in the original Hebrew means 'to give [good or bad] news,' is loaded with extra meaning. In effect, the choice of verb serves Amichai in creating the dual meaning of his statement. This use transforms the meaning of the word from its concrete sense of 'announcing' a simple message to its abstract meaning of giving a more meaningful message.

The next sentence creates an analogy between the loudspeaker as a modern technical instrument and its counterpart on the more sacred level – the rams' horns, the *shofars*, which are sounded on Rosh Hashanah, the Jewish High Holy Days. This type of built-in analogy is found also in Amichai's poetry. It intends to reduce the sacred into its secular components, or to negate past and present, the lofty and the mundane, the concrete with the abstract, and vice versa.

In so doing, Amichai reproduces the ironical effect that typifies the Jewish condition in modern times. His language and style blur the sacred and the secular into a contradictory cohesiveness.

This text is not without a reference to the Holocaust, which is enhanced in the next statement. The silence of the sacred rams' horns gets a blunt theological meaning, a powerful, yet painful, post-Holocaust vocal protestation against the Almighty.

The third statement, which appears to be an explanatory sentence, does not follow logically the previous two sentences. For if every day is indeed a day of decision, the rams' horns should be blown every day, and there is no reason for their silence. "Day of decision" is the English rendering of "day of judgment" in Hebrew – "*yom hadin*" – which is another term referring to Rosh Hashanah. The High Holy Days in the Jewish tradition are considered to be days of judgment.

However, the day of judgment in the train stations, as "The trains had left on their way" (p. 58), is but an allusion that goes back to the transportation of Jews to the death camps during the war years. The "last shipment of Jews from Weinburg" as they "waited at the station" is cited by the first-person narrator in the Weinburg scene (p. 80). Another reference cites the railroad tracks on which the Jews were sent to the death camps (p. 105). Thus, the silence of the rams' horns – the means of communicating with the Almighty – is a bitter metaphor for the enigmatic silence of God, in the believers' view, during the Shoah.

Amichai's style is saturated with inner allusions and clues, referring again and again to the issues which he deals with thematically. His style enriches and intensifies the contents and highlights recurring motifs in a manner that bonds various segments of the novel into a meaningful, unified, and continuous structure.

Structure

The structure of the novel is divided into two planes, with the Jerusalem segments on one level and the Weinburg segments on the other. The two sets, totaling sixty-eight chapters, follow consecutively from one *mise en scène* to another, from Jerusalem to Weinburg and back to Jerusalem. Consecutive chapters are attached to each other and follow one another. The two sets have parallel events, characters, and symbols, as will be discussed below, which unite the two levels into a flowing continuity of a somewhat single plot despite the ostensible geographic gap between them and the complexity and length of the novel. Amichai structured his novel cleverly so that each level of the plot is interrelated to the other.

To facilitate this technique, Amichai created parallel events in the two levels of the novel. Even though he is split between the levels, Joel in the Jerusalem scene, who becomes the first-person narrator in the Weinburg scene, is never detached from his experiences on the second level of the story. As though perceived subconsciously, identical events occur on both levels. Thus, for example, the first-person narrator in Germany remembers "the face of the strange woman in Zeiger's showcase" in Jerusalem (pp. 74, 96).

And in order to have a continuum between the two levels of the story, that is, between the events in Jerusalem and those in Weinburg in the chapter that follows, Amichai creates natural transitions between them. It is done to avoid an abrupt shift from one geographic location to another, from one scene to another. Also, it helps to create a continuous flow of plot in each level as it detaches and the scene moves to the following chapter with its own flowing plot and its previous continuum.

Thus, chapter 8 in Weinburg ends at night ("it gets dark," p. 36) while chapter 9, in Jerusalem, begins in the evening (p. 37). And then, chapter 10, continuing the story from chapter 8, also takes place at the end of the afternoon as it gets dark ("when it got dark," p. 38).

The continuity of the plot between chapters on one level, for example between chapters 9 and 11, is also maintained by some reference. Chapter 9 ends with the bell ringing (p. 38) and it continues in chapter 11 with the ringing of the bell (p. 41). Similarly, chapter 56 ends with the death of Dr. Manheim, and chapter 57 begins with the death of Henrietta (p. 280). And another example: chapter 63 ends with the biblical quotation "My God, my God, why have You forsaken me?" and chapter 64 opens with the same quotation on the other plane of the novel (p. 308).

It should be noted that as a result of the abridgement in the English edition of the novel (from 86 to 68 chapters), some chapters or segments have been eliminated, thus affecting this continuity. For example, chapter 44 ends with the prayer "Our Father, Our King," which is cited in the next chapter in Hebrew, but that paragraph has been eliminated in English in the beginning of chapter 45 (p. 216).

These literary techniques, which relate segments of the plot externally, intrinsically touch the very essence of the novel, namely Joel's attitude toward the Holocaust. They emphasize the notion that Joel's obsession with the Holocaust is related to the duality of his persona and his experiences on the two levels of the novel, in Weinburg and in Jerusalem. Joel's problem is related to the fact that he had not experienced the Holocaust on his own person, yet he is attached by psychological and emotional roots to its victims. He cannot make peace with himself until he comes to grips with this dilemma that confronts him. Joel feels guilty because he was spared, and it is mixed with a desire for vengeance, which turns out to be an obsession.

Little Ruth and Her Sufferings

Amichai's use of the connecting devices between the two plots extends beyond techniques which may seem to be mechanical and artificial; at times they reach the level of symbols. Case in point is the use of the very powerful image of little Ruth that appears also in Amichai's poems and short stories. Little Ruth is a figure from the protagonist's childhood in Germany. Her leg was amputated after an accident, and she was given a wooden leg. Finally, her fate was the same as the other Jews, and both she and the wooden leg were burned in the Holocaust. Now, the split-person Joel, in his role as the first-person narrator, is looking for her on the German soil after he had tried to find a substitute for her in the figure of his own wife whose name is also Ruth. The narrator clearly states that Joel "loved his wife Ruth, who bore the name of little Ruth from his childhood days. And this was no accident" (p. 6). Joel, the narrator continues, "always carried his entire life within himself" – "all his memories, his childhood, his encounters, his conflicts, little Ruth and his wife Ruth" (p. 7).

In a dream, Joel sees little Ruth playing with him in Weinburg, and then she accuses him, in his own mind, saying, "You always look for comfort [...]. You even married a wife named Ruth so you should be comfortable and easy" (p. 8). The two aspects of Joel's life, being both Israeli and German-born, are exemplified by the dual namesake 'Ruth,' and he is torn between them: "He was confused by the thoughts of little Ruth from his childhood and of his wife Ruth, who came from a kibbutz" (p. 11). He then reaches a decision to go back to Weinburg, the city of his childhood in Germany, where "he wanted to be with his little dead Ruth" (p. 9). "What would I do there?" Joel asks himself, and he replies, "Perhaps I'll avenge little Ruth, Manheim's daughter, whom the people of Weinburg sent to the crematorium" (p. 13).

The image of little Ruth continues to haunt him, and the ambiguity about her image persists in his mind. It is exemplified in the scene in which Joel's mother scolds him, "Why are you so mean to Ruth?" And Joel does not know which Ruth she meant, whether "my wife Ruth or little Ruth who was burned in a crematorium" (p. 24).

The references to little Ruth abound in the novel, continuously building her image in relation to Joel and in his emblematic perception of her and of himself.

The name 'Ruth' was purposefully selected because it alludes to the biblical figure of Ruth. It was Ruth who expressed her wish to join another people in a supreme gesture of loyalty as recorded in the Bible in this memorable statement: "...Your people shall be my people, and your God my God..." (*Ruth* 1:16). Emulating the biblical Ruth, little Ruth is indeed a representation of German Jewry that, since the end of the eighteenth century, expressed its loyalty to the German people, adhered and contributed to its culture, and some even adopted its faith.

In spite of the Jewish active participation in German society and culture, the recollected story of little Ruth in her Germanic surrounding depicts the rise of Nazism and some other aspects of the history of German Jewry. One such experience from his childhood is recalled by the first-person narrator: "Once, she and I were knocked down by Nazi boys" (p. 52).

Going back to the past, in a chapter that was omitted in the English version,[6] Joel accuses the German priest who caused the accident that he was to blame for little Ruth's death. Extending beyond the confines of the story, this accusation has relevance in the context of the history of the Holocaust. It is here that Amichai is referring to the role of the church in classical anti-Semitism, which led eventually, directly or indirectly, to the Shoah. The priest also admits that every German participated in the persecution of Jews and in their deportation (p. 514, in Hebrew). Finally, he is found dead, floating on the river (p. 574, in Hebrew), and thus he is punished for his deed (as will be discussed later with regard to the skull floating on the river).

Alluding to little Ruth's end, the narrator relates that following the accident, little Ruth's leg was amputated; however, he adds sarcastically, her leg was burned several years before they burned the rest of her body:

---

6.   See original Hebrew, Amichai, *Lo Me'achshav Lo Mikan*, p. 516; in the English version, it was supposed to be in chapter 55.

...two men must have approached Ruth when she was being led to the crematorium [...]. Ruth was badly in need of heavenly assistance and must have been helped by someone nearby as she skipped on one foot, for she had no doubt already been deprived of her crutch. Little Ruth had known many sorrows long before the troubles descended on everyone else. Her leg, which she had lost in an accident, had been burned long before the rest of her body (p. 61).

It is a cruel expression of the maltreatment of German Jewry long before Nazism came to power and afterwards.

Vengeance

The figure of little Ruth serves as a focal point for developing the central theme of vengeance in the novel. Joel decides to go to Weinburg "to find burned little Ruth" (p. 18). The original Hebrew is more definite, specifying that Joel was going to Weinburg "to redeem" little Ruth (p. 25, in Hebrew).

The first-person narrator asks himself about the purpose of his "returning" to Weinburg, and he answers, "It began with a dream and grew with a great longing for a lost childhood. Now all these feelings have merged into a passion to avenge what they had done to little Ruth" (p. 36).

Undoubtedly, vengeance is one of the central themes of the novel, a theme that prevailed in the post-war milieu and is reflected in the post-Holocaust literature. Actually, Amichai described an attempt at vengeance, an attempt that has failed. This desire for vengeance is tied to the image of little Ruth as perceived by the protagonist's desire to go back to the place of his childhood. His attitude toward the past also raises the issue of his remembrance and forgetfulness vis-à-vis the Shoah.

Amichai delineated the protagonist's consciousness and the gradual changes that he undergoes regarding the question of vengeance and his ability actually to perform it.

As the protagonist, and the plot, move toward the target of Weinburg, changes occur. In the first part of the novel, up to chapter 8, there is a growing desire on the part of the first-person narrator to avenge his childhood friend, little Ruth.

In the second part of the novel (chapters 8 and on), with the shift of the plot to Europe and as Joel moves on toward Weinburg, there is some hesitation on the part of the protagonist. On his way to Weinburg, Joel is still unsure within himself whether he should or should not go to Weinburg, saying, "I thought, as I usually do, I will stay here; I will not go back to Weinburg to close the door on my longings; I will not take vengeance; I will stay here..." (p. 36).

His hesitancy further increases as he now debates about the nature of this possible vengeance. He asks himself whether he should come to Weinburg "with the sadness of an adult who returns to the scenes of his childhood, or should I burst into it like an avenging god?" (p. 40).

But when he returns to the world of his childhood, he realizes that he made a mistake by placing his wish for vengeance solely on the issue of little Ruth. He now realizes that she is still 'alive' – a reference to the small surviving Jewish community in Germany and to some Jews who returned to Germany, reflecting the situation in the 1950s and 1960s. Joel finds them as he visits the old age home, and sees them in their dying stages. "I made a big mistake when I placed my vengeance totally on avenging little Ruth. Now, that she is alive, what should I do," the first-person narrator asks himself, "[now that] the ground has slipped under my [desire for] vengeance?" This part, unfortunately, was eliminated from the English translation.[7]

...And Hate

As Amichai delineates the character of Joel, he examines his motivation for vengeance. He depicts Joel's coming to Weinburg "on account of hate" (p. 87). But, typically, Joel is indecisive about the reason to avenge little Ruth, saying to himself, "I thought, How will I hate? I sank into my memories as one sinks into forgetfulness. Time was passing and I still didn't hate" (p. 88).

In this literary representation of the desire to avenge as based on hate, the protagonist is unable to develop his hate which seems to be a prerequisite of vengeance; thus, the desire for vengeance does not materialize. As portrayed by Amichai, sinking into his memories – namely, going back to his childhood in Germany – is comparable to sinking into forgetfulness, which annuls any possibility of hatred. Joel admits,

Standing thus, I was not an avenger; I was like any other man who returns to the landscape of his childhood. My vengeance was like a wax sword. A great sadness descended upon me because I was empty of vengeance, for it was for its sake that I had come here all the way from Jerusalem... (p. 106).

The third part of the novel (chapters 55 and on) highlights the change that had taken place in Joel's ethical stand vis-à-vis the Shoah.

Joel's change of heart and his moral impotence are explained by two critics of Hebrew literature, Baruch Kurzweil and Hillel Barzel, as related to

---

7. *Ibid*, p. 488.

his profession as an archaeologist, which leads him to despair, indecisiveness, lack of established values, and relativity.[8]

Joel's moral stand is ambivalent; he cannot establish ethical rules regarding righteous people and wicked ones (p. 549, in Hebrew). His moral stand is compromised also as a result of his intimacy with Patricia, who is not Jewish, in the Jerusalem part of the novel. Thus, he is apparently unable to identify totally with the fate of the Jewish dead. Joel's inability to avenge little Ruth because of his identity with the place of his childhood results in immobility to act violently or to act at all.

As an archaeologist, he may even accept what his Indian friend told him about the historical summation of the Holocaust:

> Our memory tells us that the Nazis had murdered so-and-so many Jews and that the city was destroyed by the American army. Crime and punishment. History will describe the events otherwise. It will say: 'So-and-so many Jews and Germans were killed in the great war.' Here will be a balancing and equalizing of oppressed and oppressors. More distant history, which has to embrace many generations and wars, will say: 'In the middle of the twentieth century a great war raged and so-and-so many people perished in it.' Archeology of times to come will define the events as follows: 'It appears that toward the end of the second millennium or the beginning of the third millennium of the Christian era a great catastrophe occurred marked by many conflagrations. This is proved by a black, fire-scorched layer and numerous broken iron objects that have been uncovered. The city appears to have been rebuilt' (p. 295).

Joel's historical-archaeological point of view, which typifies not only his profession but his personality as well, is at the core of his inability to act. Furthermore, his Jerusalem experience annuls any possible emotional attachment to the reality on the German level of the novel.

A Skull Floating on the Water

The notion of vengeance is exemplified by the central motif of a skull floating on the water.[9]

This motif appears in the Jerusalem scene with Patricia, Joel's Christian friend. The narrator describes Joel shaving: "In the mirror he saw her head

---

8. Baruch Kurzweil, "Notes on '*Lo Me'achshav Lo Mikan*' by Y. Amichai," *Haaretz* Literary Supplement, September 6, 1963, September 13, 1963 [Hebrew]. Hillel Barzel, [Review of '*Lo Me'achshav Lo Mikan*'] in *Moznayim*, 17 (No. 4–5, 1963), pp. 497–501 [Hebrew]; Barzel, *Metarealistic Hebrew Prose* (Ramat Gan, 1974), chapter on Amichai, pp. 70–84 [Hebrew].

9. It is more visible in the original Hebrew than in the English translation where many of the references have been omitted.

above the water, her eyes closed, and he whispered to himself, 'Because you love you shall be loved, and in the end your lovers will drown'" (p. 290).

It is a parodic reference to the story in *The Ethics of the Fathers* (*Pirkei Avot*) about the sage Hillel who was walking on a road next to a river. He saw a skull floating on the water and he said to it, "For drowning others thou wast drowned."[10] The interpretation of this proverbial story is that it was the skull of a highway robber who killed people and finally got his punishment.[11] However, the Jewish sage goes on further to say that those who drowned the robber (perhaps without a court's judgment) will be punished as well.

This is the classical notion of reward and punishment and of eventual justice, perhaps vengeance. However, in its parodic, albeit meaningful, presentation, Joel is taking the same linguistic structure of the classical phrase and converts it, through Amichai's style of manipulation, to the context of the novel. Namely, because you love, as Joel did, you were loved, but at the end the lovers will have the same fate as in the classical, paradigmatic story: they will meet their end. By superimposing the classical structure on his modern statement but ending it with the classical punishment, Amichai conveys the notion that love and vengeance are intertwined in the story.

Indeed, the idea of Jewish vengeance, symbolized by the skull, is cancelled by Joel's love for Patricia. Joel considers the end of his love and the end of his vengeance as his own demise.

Joel, then, reaches the moral conclusion that "there is no reward and there is no punishment; there is no act of love and there is no act of vengeance, and there is not going back but only a rolling of skulls floating on the flowing river." This conclusion of the first-person narrator's statement was omitted from the English (p. 541 in the Hebrew, around chapter 6 in the English). Similarly, there are some additional references to the skull in other chapters of both the Jerusalem and the German segments which allude to the message in the classical story of the skull. Some of the references are cited sporadically, almost incidentally, such as in the following example: "Joel turned on the light, which was inside a skull" (p. 103). Some references may serve as a parody on this motif, as in the episode with the border warning sign where "Vicky added a mustache and glasses to the skull" (p. 97). Another reference in the Weinburg scene picks up one aspect of the skull story, such as the river, and compares it to the

---

10. *Pirkei Avot*, chapter 2, v. 6. This phrase is used as a motto to the Hebrew edition. See similar discussion in the chapter on Ka-tzetnik.

11. Another interpretation relates it to the reign of King Herod in the first century BCE.

instrument which transported the Jews to their death, namely the trains: "During the war they didn't take people to their death on this river, because it flows west. It is therefore innocent, unlike the railroad tracks that go east" (p. 105).

Shimeon Zandbank, an Israeli critic, concluded that "'for drowning' is interpreted paradoxically as a slogan of an endless and amoral flow, without reward or punishment [...]. The flowing river in which the skulls float symbolizes [...] the type of existence which is beyond decision."[12] Joel says, "I love the river also because it flows and does make decision" (in the Hebrew).

Remembering and Forgetting

Joel's desire for vengeance and his inability to act on it are related to his vacillation between remembering and forgetting. This psychological fluctuation is also described by Amichai in its gradual development, similar to the desire for revenge. For Joel, love may be a vehicle for forgetting: "If I were deeply in love, this would be the right time to forget. Forgetting a door is the same as closing it, the same as forgetting the future, as forgetting the past" (p. 59). At times it appears that he would not be able to forget:

Now I have lost my last chance to forget. From now on I won't be able to forget. There is a time for remembering and a time for forgetting, a time for opening doors and a time for locking them. But with the last chance to forget gone, all the details came to life within me (p. 96).

The relativity of remembering and forgetting is highlighted by Amichai as he uses a play on words and contradiction, saying that he remembers the forgetfulness and this in effect is remembering (p. 244, in Hebrew). In what appears to be a revealing statement on the relativity of these concepts, the narrator questions the reliability of memory, saying that all memories in effect cause to forget the truth... (p. 37, in Hebrew).

These references were omitted from the English, important as they are to understand the position of the non-survivor author in the post-Holocaust era. Amichai highlights the problematics of the Israeli, and for that matter also the Jew, in the post-Holocaust era. It seems that those who have not experienced the Shoah on their own selves, their 'remembering' is not authentic as they don't remember the very experience of the Holocaust but remember a story, the story told by others. And in as much as the survivor's remembering is true and is based on experience, it cannot be directly conveyed to outsiders as 'memories' of the Holocaust.

---

12. Shimeon Zandbank, [Review of Amichai's novel], *Amot*, II (No. 8, October-November, 1963), pp. 97–101 [Hebrew].

The biblical command "*Zachor!*" (" Thou shall remember") demands of whoever practices it to believe in Jewish values. Yet, it appears that Joel is far from it. The Israeli critic Hillel Barzel dealt with this topic, asserting that vengeful Joel underwent the same process that Amichai's processes of linguistic association exhibit, resulting in a complete reduction of values of traditional Judaism.[13]

Therefore, the external symmetry in the novel, the parallels in the plots, and the other connecting elements are to be construed as an illusion of some harmony. The structural concept of the novel and its author is ironic in that it does not believe in the perfect order of things, nor in their harmony. Amichai builds structures in order to destroy them, as he has done with his linguistic structures: debasing the sacred and highlighting paradoxes, contradictions, and incongruities.

Joel, the Israeli, was destined to be doomed, but his counterpart, product of the *Galut*, the state of exile, returns from Germany to Israel not sure whether his life will be "stormy and fateful, or calm with endless peaceful thoughts" (p. 344).

---

13. Barzel's article appeared in *Moznayim*, 17 (No. 4-5, September-October, 1963), pp. 497–501.

Bibliography

Studied Texts

Amichai, Yehuda. *Lo Me'achshav Lo Mikan* [Not from Now Not from Here]. Jerusalem & Tel Aviv, 1963.
—. *Not of This Time, Not of This Place.* New York, 1968. Trans. by Shlomo Katz.
Appelfeld, Aharon. *Badenheim 1939.* Boston, 1980; New York, 1981. Trans. by Dalia Bilu.
—. "Badenheim, Ir Nofesh" [Badenheim, a Resort Town], *Shanim Vesha'ot* [Years and Hours]. Israel, 1975, pp. 5–103 [Hebrew].
Bartov, Hanoch. *The Brigade.* Philadelphia, 1968.
—. *Pitz'ei Bagrut* [Acnes; Wounds of Maturity]. Tel Aviv, 1965 [Hebrew].
Gouri, Haim. *The Chocolate Deal.* New York, 1968; Detroit, 1999; with an introduction by Geoffrey Hartman. Trans. by Seymour Simckes.
—. *Iskat Hashokolad* [The Chocolate Deal]. Tel Aviv, 1965.
Ka-tzetnik, *Kochav Ha'efer* [Star of Ash]. Israel, 1966 [Hebrew].
—. Ka-tzetnik 135633. *Star Eternal.* New York, 1971.
Kosinski, Jerzy. *The Painted Bird.* Boston, 1975; New York, 1995.
Levi, Primo. *Survival in Auschwitz.* New York, 1996.
Wiesel, Elie. *Night.* New York, 1969; New York, 1982.

Selected Books and Articles

Adorno, Theodor W. *Noten zur Literatur, Gesammelte Schriften,* II. Frankfurt A/M, 1974.
—. *Notes to Literature,* II. New York, 1992.
Agnon, S. Y. *Twenty One Stories.* New York, 1971.

131

Alexander, Edward. "The Destruction and Resurrection of the Jews in the Fiction of I. B. Singer," *Judaism*, XXV (No. 1, Winter 1976), pp. 98–106.

—. "The Holocaust in American-Jewish Fiction: A Slow Awakening," *Judaism*, XXV (No. 3, Summer 1976), pp. 320–330.

—. *The Resonance of Dust*. Columbus, 1979.

Alter, Robert. *After the Tradition*. New York, 1960.

—. "Confronting the Holocaust", *After the Tradition*. New York, 1960, pp. 163–180.

—. "Elie Wiesel: Between Hangman and Victim," *After the Tradition*. New York, 1960, pp. 151–160.

Alvarez, A. "The Literature of the Holocaust," *Commentary* (November 1964), pp. 65–69.

—. "The Literature of the Holocaust," *Beyond All This Fiddle* [:] Essays 1955-1967. New York, 1968.

Appelfeld, Aharon. "Bertha," in *Facing the Holocaust*, Gila Ramras-Rauch, Joseph Michman-Melkman, ed. Philadelphia, 1985, pp. 143–159.

—. "Ha'eimah Vehahit'hayvut" [Horror and Commitment], *Ma'ariv* Literary Supplement, August 8, 1975.

—. *In the Wilderness: Stories*. Jerusalem, 1965.

—. *Masot Beguf Rishon* [Essay in First Person]. Jerusalem, 1979.

—. [Review of Primo Levi's book], *Sfarim* Literary Supplement of *Haaretz* Daily, September 25, 2002 [Hebrew].

Bartov, Omer. *Murder in Our Midst [:] The Holocaust, Industrial Killing, and Representation*. New York, 1996.

Barzel, Hillel. *Metarealistic Hebrew Prose*. Ramat Gan, 1974. Chapter on Amichai, pp. 70–84 [Hebrew].

Bauer, Yehuda. *A History of the Holocaust*. New York, 1982.

Berger, Alan L. *Crisis and Covenant: The Holocaust in American Jewish Fiction*. Albany, 1985.

Brown, Jean E. et al., ed., *Images from the Holocaust [:] A Literature Anthology*. Lincolnwood, Il., 1997.

Cohen, Arthur Allen. *The American Imagination After the War: Notes on the Novel, Jews and Hope*. Syracuse, 1981.

Dawidowicz, Lucy S. *A Holocaust Reader*. New York, 1976.

—. *The War against the Jews 1933–1945*. New York, 1975.

Des Pres, Terrence. *The Survivor*. New York, 1976.

Eliach, Yaffa. "The Holocaust in Hebrew Drama," *Jewish Book Annual*. (Vol. 36, 1978–79), pp. 37–49.

Ezrahi, Sidra DeKoven. *By Words Alone*. Chicago & London, 1979.

Feierburg, M. Z. *Whither? And Other Stories*. Philadelphia, 1973.

Fine, Ellen S. *Legacy of Night*. Albany, 1982.

—. *The Literary Universe of Elie Wiesel*. Albany, 1982.

Gil, Moshe. [Review article on "Iskat Hashokolad" [*The Chocolate Deal*], in *Moznayim*, 20 (No. 43, December 1965–May 1965), p. 381 [Hebrew].

Ha-Kohen, Yosef. *Emek Habacha* [The Valley of Tears]. Krakau, 1895. Letteris edition [Hebrew].

Gilman, Richard. "Nat Turner Revisited," *The New Republic*, 158 (No. 17, April 27, 1968).

Glatstein, Jacob. et al., *Anthology of Holocaust Literature*. Philadelphia, 1969.

Golan, Shammai ed. *Hashoah, Pirkei Edut Vesifrut* [The Holocaust: Eye-Witness and Literary Accounts]. Tel Aviv, 1976 [Hebrew].

Goldhagen, Daniel J. *Hitler's Willing Executioners [:] Ordinary Germans and the Holocaust.* New York, 1996.

Gross, Natan, Itamar Yaoz-Kest and Rina Klinov, ed. *Hashoah Bashirah Ha'ivrit* [Holocaust in Hebrew Poetry]. Tel Aviv, 1974 [Hebrew].

H. B., "K. Tzetnik," *Keshet*, XV (No. 1, Fall 1972), pp. 188–189 [Hebrew].

Halperin, Irving. "Meaning and Despair in the Literature of the Survivors," *Jewish Book Annual*, XXVI, (1968–69), pp. 7–22.

—. *Messengers From the Dead*. Philadelphia, 1970.

Hazaz, Hayim. "Adam Miyisrael" [A Man of Israel] and "Haderashah" [The Sermon], in *Supurim Nivharim* [Select Stories]. Tel Aviv, 1952, pp. 149–157, 184–202 [Hebrew].

Heinemann, Marlene L. *Gender and Destiny: Women Writers on the Holocaust*. Westport, 1986.

Highet, Gilbert. *The Anatomy of Satire*. Princeton, 1962.

Hilberg, Raul. *The Distruction of the European Jews*. New York, 1961.

Ibn Verga, Shlomo. *Shevet Yehudah* [The Sceptre of Judah]. Jerusalem, n.d. Levin Epstein Edition [Hebrew].

Kohn, Murray J. *The Voice of My Blood Cries Out*. New York, 1979.

Korman, Gerd. ed. *Hunter and Hunted*. New York, 1973.

Konsinki, Jerzy. *Notes of the Author on The Painted Bird*. New York, 1967.

Langer, Lawrence L. *The Age of Atrocity [:] Death in Modern Literature*. Boston, 1978.

—. *The Holocaust and the Literary Imagination*. New Haven, 1975.

—. *Preempting the Holocaust*. New Haven, 1998.

—. *Versions of Survival, The Holocaust and the Human Spirit*. Albany, 1982.

Levi, Primo. "Author's Preface," *Survival in Auschwitz*. New York, 1996.

Levin, Nora. *The Holocaust [:] The Destruction of European Jewry 1933–1945*. New York, 1973.

Lewis, Stephen. *Art Out of Agony, The Holocaust Theme in Literature, Sculpture and Film*. Montreal & New York, 1984.

Meucke, D. C. *The Compass of Irony*. London, n.d.

Mintz, Alan L. *Hurban: Responses to Catastrophe in Hebrew Literature.* New York, 1984.

Morgan, Michael, L. *A Holocaust Reader [:] Responses to the Nazi Extermination.* New York & Oxford, 2001.

Ovadyahu, Mordechai. *Besa'ar Uvidemamah* [In Storm and Silence]. Tel Aviv, 1976 [Hebrew].

Patterson, David. *The Shreik of Silence [:] A Phenomenology of the Holocaust Novel.* Lexington, 1992.

Pelli, Moshe. "Elie Wiesel: The Right to Question," *Melbourne Chronicle.* (March–April, 1979), pp. 12–15.

—. "Elie Wiesel: Zechut Hashe'elah," *Bitzaron*, XXXVIII (Adar–Nisan, 1978), pp. 294–298 [Hebrew].

—. "Erev Hasho'ah Beroman Hadash Shel Bashevis Singer," *Hadoar*, LVIII (No. 4, November 24, 1978), pp. 58–59 [Hebrew].

—. "Hanefesh Hamefutzelet Bimetzi'ut Hatzuyah Le'ahar Hashoah," *Hadoar*, LVIII (No. 30, June 22, 1979), p. 492; (No. 31, June 1979), p. 509 [Hebrew].

—. "Hidalon Ve'ashlayah Beterem Sho'ah," *Hadoar*, LX (No. 20, March 27, 1981), pp. 312–313 [Hebrew].

—. "Tefisat Hametzi'ut Habetar Sho'atit Beroman Shel Hayim Gouri," *Hadoar*, LVII (No. 25, May 5, 1978), pp. 413–415 [Hebrew].

Ramras-Rauch, Gila. *Aharon Appelfeld: The Holocaust and Beyond.* Bloomington, 1994.

Ramras-Rauch, Gila and Joseph Michman-Melkman, ed., *Facing the Holocaust: Selected Israeli Fiction*, with an introduction by G. Ramras-Rauch and afterword by Gershon Shaked. Philadelphia, 1985.

Resnais, Alain, director. *Nait et Brouillard* [Night and Fog], filmed in 1955.

Rosen, Norma. "The Holocaust and the American-Jewish Novelist," *Midstream*, XX (No. 8, October 1974), pp. 54–62.

Rosenfeld, Alvin. *A Double Dying [:] Reflections on Holocaust Literature.* Bloomington, 1980.

—. *Imagining Hitler.* Bloomington, 1985.

Rosenfeld, Alvin and Irving Greenberg, ed. *Confronting the Holocaust: The Impact of Elie Wiesel.* Bloomington, 1978.

Roskies, David G. *Against the Apocalypse: Responses to Catastrophe in Modern Jewish Culture.* Cambridge, 1984.

—. *The Literature of Destruction [:] Jewish Responses to Catastrophe.* Philadelphia, 1989.

Roth, John K. and Michael Berenbaum, ed. *Holocaust [:] Religious and Philosophical Implications.* New York, 1989.

Rousset, David. *The Other Kingdom.* New York, 1982 [English translation of *L'univers Concentrationnaire.* Paris, 1946].

Schwartz, Yigal. *Individual Lament and Tribal Eternity.* Jerusalem, 1996 [Hebrew].

Shaked, Gershon. "Childhood Lost, Studies in the Holocaust Themes in Contemporary Israeli Fiction," *Literature East and West,* XIV (No. 1, March), pp. 90–108.

—. "Facing the Nightmare: Israeli Literature on the Holocaust," *Facing the Holocaust.* Philadelphia, 1985, pp. 273–288.

—. *Gal Hadash Basiporet Ha'ivrit* [A New Wave in Hebrew Fiction]. Tel Aviv, 1971 [Hebrew].

Steiner, George. *Language and Silence.* New York, 1967.

—. [Article], *Commentary,* Vol. 39 (No. 2, February 1965), p. 32.

Stern, David. "Imagining the Holocaust," *Commentary,* 62 (No. 1, July 1976), pp. 46–51.

Weiss, Hillel. *Dyoqan Halohem* [Profile of the Fighter]. Ramat Gan, 1975 [Hebrew].

Wyman, David S. *The Abandonment of the Jews.* New York, 1984–5.

Yahil, Leni. *The Holocaust [:] The Fate of European Jewry.* New York, 1991.

Young, James E. *The Texture of Memory.* New Haven, 1993.

—. *Writing and Rewriting the Holocaust.* Bloomington, 1990.

Yudkin, Leon I. "Appelfeld's Vision of the Past," *Escape into Siege.* London & Boston, 1974, pp. 116–123.

—. "The Israeli Writer and the Holocaust," *Ibid.,* pp. 124–134.

Yuter, Alan J. *The Holocaust in Hebrew Literature, From Genocide to Rebirth.* Port Washington, N.Y., 1983.

Authors' and Artists' Biographies

Aharon Appelfeld (1932-) An Israeli novelist, survivor of the Holocaust. Born in Czernowitz, Rumania, Appelfeld immigrated to Israel in 1946. He is the author of over 30 books of novels and short stories. Written in Hebrew, his works have been translated into many languages. Appelfeld was Professor of Hebrew Literature at Ben Gurion University of the Negev. He was awarded the Israel Prize for literature in 1983 and several other literary prizes as well as honorary degrees. His first book, *Smoke* (short stories), was published in 1962; since then he has continued to publish novels that center on the Jewish experience in Europe around the time of World War II. Among his novels available in English translation: *The Age of Wonders* (1981), *Tzili* (1983), *Katerina* (1992), *Iron Tracks* (1998), and *The Conversion* (1999).

Elie Wiesel (1928-) An American Jewish novelist, survived the Auschwitz and Buchenwald death camps, born in Sighet, Transylvania. After the liberation he went to France. He became a journalist, writing for newspapers in France, Israel, and the U.S. (New York). Since 1976 he has been the Andrew Mellon Professor of Humanities at Boston University. He has lived in New York since the mid 1950s. In the 1960s Wiesel became active on behalf of persecuted Jews in the Soviet Union. He traveled to the U.S.S.R. in 1965 and reported on Russian Jewry in *The Jews of Silence*. In 1980 he was appointed to chair the President's Commission on the Holocaust, which led to the establishment of the Holocaust Museum in Washington. In 1985 he was awarded the Congressional Gold Medal of Achievement, and in 1986 he was awarded the Nobel Peace Prize. The Nobel Committee called him a "messenger to mankind" for bringing the Holocaust to the attention of the world. He has been given many other awards and honorary doctorate degrees. Wiesel has been an advocate of human rights for many years. He wrote over forty books, among them, *Night* (1958), *Dawn* (1961), *Day* (previously titled *The Accident*, 1962), *The Town Beyond the Wall* (1964), *The Gates of the Forest* (1966), *Four Hasidic Masters* (1978), *Images from the Bible* (1980), *Wise Men and Their Tales* (2003), *The Time of the Uprooted* (2005). His books have been translated into many languages.

Primo Levi (1919–1987) A Jewish Italian author, Holocaust survivor of Auschwitz, born in Turin, Italy. Levi wrote fifteen books of memoirs, short stories, poems, essays, and novels. His most known books which have been translated into English are *If This Is a Man* (*Survival in Auschwitz*) (1958) and *The Truce* or *The Reawakening* (1965). *If This Is a Man* is considered to be one of the most important works of twentieth century literature. Levi has been recognized as a major writer in Italy and abroad. His books were translated into many languages. *If Not Now, When?* (1982) won several Italian literary prizes.

Ka-tzetnik (1909–2001) An Israeli writer, survivor of Auschwitz. He documented Nazi atrocities under the pen name Ka-tzetnik 135633 (K.Z., pronounced: Kah-Tzet, an abbreviation of Konzentration Zentrum, and his tattooed number). Born Yehiel Feiner in Sosnowiec, Poland, he changed his name to Dinur (meaning "of the fire" in Aramaic). In 1945 he came to pre-state Israel. He was one of the first to write of his own experiences in the Holocaust, writing under the pseudonym. His identity was revealed when he testified at the Eichmann trial in 1961. Among his translated books: *The House of Dolls* (published in Hebrew in 1956), *Atrocity, Star Eternal* (published in Hebrew in 1966), and *Piepel*.

Jerzy Kosinski (1933–1991) A Jewish Polish-American novelist. Born Josek Lewinkopf in Lodz, Poland, he survived the war under a false identity as a Roman Catholic. He immigrated to the United States in 1957 and was a lecturer at Yale and other universities. Among his ten novels: *The Painted Bird* (1965), which received an award in France for best foreign work of fiction, *Steps* (1969), which received the National Book Award, *Being There* (1971), which was made into an Oscar-winning movie in 1979, and *Cockpit* (1975). The publication of *The Painted Bird* brought about a bitter debate, although Elie Wiesel hailed it as "One of the best [...]. Written with deep sincerity and sensitivity" (in *The New York Times Book Reviews*).

Hanoch Bartov (1926-   ) An Israeli novelist, born in Petah Tikva in pre-state Israel. In 1943, at age 17, he enlisted in the Palestine Regiment of the British Army, serving in the Jewish Brigade for three years. In Israel's War of Independence he served in the Israeli Defense Forces. He was a journalist and foreign correspondent for several newspapers, and from 1966 to 1968 he served as cultural advisor in the Israeli embassy in London. He published about thirty books of fiction, short stories and non-fiction, and received several literary awards, among them the Bialik Prize in 1985. Among his books published in English: *The Brigade* (1967), translation of *Pitz'ei Bagrut* (1965), *Everyone Had Six Wings* (1974), translation of *Shesh Kenafaim Le-Ehad* (1954), *An Israeli at the Court of St. James* (1971), *Whose Little Boy Are You?* (1978), translation of *Shel Mi Ata Yeled* (1970), and *Dado, 48 Years 20 Days* (1981).

Hayim Gouri (1923-) An Israeli poet, novelist and journalist, born in Tel Aviv. After World War II, he helped Jews immigrate to pre-state Israel. He fought in the 1948 Israel's War of Independence, and is highly esteemed as the poet of the 1948 generation. Many of his poems were set to music and became popular songs. Among other prizes, he was awarded the Bialik Prize for Literature in 1975 and the Israel Prize for Poetry in 1988. The film *The 81st Blow*, which he wrote, co-produced, and co-directed, was nominated for the 1974 Academy Award for Documentary Feature. He wrote twenty books, twelve of which are collected poems. Among his books in poetry: *Flowers of Fire, Years of Fire* (1949), *Poems of the Seal* (1954), *Compass Rose* (1960), *Words in My Love-Sick Blood* (1996; selected poems in English translation), *The Poems* (1998). Fiction titles: *The Chocolate Deal* (1965; English translation: 1968, 1999), *The Crazy Book* (1971). Non-fiction titles: *Facing the Glass Booth: the Jerusalem Trial of Adolf Eichmann* (1962; English translation: 2004).

Yehuda Amichai (1924–2000) An Israeli poet, born in Würzburg, Germany. He immigrated with his family to pre-state Israel in 1936. He fought in World War II in the Jewish Brigade, and in Israel's War of Independence. Amichai is considered by many to be one of the most important modern Israeli poets. Many of his poems were set to music and made into popular songs. He was awarded the Bialik Prize for literature in 1976 and the Israel Prize for his poetic work in 1982. Among his books of poetry that were translated into English: *A Life of Poetry, 1948-1994* (1994), *Amen* (1977), *Even a Fist Was Once an Open Palm with Fingers: Recent Poems* (1991), *Exile at Home* (1998), *Great Tranquility: Questions and Answers* (1983), *Love Poems: A Bilingual Edition* (1981), *Open Closed Open: Poems* (2000) (Shortlisted for the 2001 International Griffin Poetry Prize). In prose: *Not of This Time, Not of This Place* (1968).

Shmuel Bak (1933-) A Jewish artist, born in Vilna, Lithuania, survived ghetto and work-camp during the war. He immigrated to Israel in 1948. Bak also lived in Paris, Rome, New York, and, since 1993, in Massachusetts. He has been exhibited in numerous galleries and museums, and his works are found in public collections in several countries. Some twelve books on, and by, the artist and his work have been published. Among them: *New Perceptions of Old Appearances in the Art of Samuel Bak* (2005), *Between Worlds: The Paintings and Drawings of Samuel Bak from 1946-2001* (2002), *Painted in Words: A Memoir* (2001), *In A Different Light: Genesis in the Art of Samuel Bak* (2001), *Landscapes of Jewish Experience* (1997), *Samuel Bak, The Past Continues* (1988).

Mordechai Goldfarb (1918–1984) An Israeli artist, born in Piaski, Poland. Goldfarb survived and escaped the concentration camp Sobibor in the uprising. He became a partisan, was recruited after the war by the Polish police, and helped rescue Jewish children from monasteries. He came to Israel in 1949. He painted and his work has been exhibited in Haifa, Israel.

About the Author

Moshe Pelli is the Abe and Tess Wise Endowed Professor in Judaic Studies and Director of the Judaic Studies Program at the University of Central Florida in Orlando, Florida. Professor Pelli is a leading authority on the Hebrew Enlightenment (Haskalah) in the eighteenth and nineteenth centuries. He has published extensively on modern Hebrew literature and on the literature of the Holocaust. Among his writings are ten scholarly books on Hebrew Enlightenment (see below), one book on Hebrew culture in America, and over 166 research papers, two novels, and eight children's books. In 1991 he was awarded the Friedman Prize for his long-time contributions to Hebrew Culture in the U.S. in the areas of teaching, research and editing Hebrew periodicals. In 1996 and 2006 he received the Researcher of the Year award at University of Central Florida. In 2007 he was elected President of the National Association of Professors of Hebrew in the United States.

Books by the Author

Haskalah and Modernity: Beginnings and Continuity – The Reception of the Early Haskalah in the 19th Century. Israel, Hakibutz Hame'uchad Publishers, Hillal ben Hayim Library: 2007 [Hebrew].

The Age of Haskalah: Studies in Hebrew Literature of the Enlightenment in Germany, Lanham, University Press of America: 2006 [Updated, revised edition].

In Search of Genres: Hebrew Enlightenment and Modernity – An Analytical Study of Literary Genres in 18th- and 19th-Century Hebrew Enlightenment. Lanham, University Press of America: 2005.

Bikurei Ha'itim The 'First Fruits' of Haskalah: An Annotated Index to *Bikurei Ha'itim*, the Hebrew Journal of the Haskalah in Galicia (1820-1831). Jerusalem, Israel, The Hebrew University Magnes Press: 2005 [Hebrew].

The Circle of Hame'asef *Writers at the Dawn of Haskalah:* The Literary Contribution of the Writers of *Hame'asef*, the First Hebrew Periodical 1783-1811. Israel, Hakibutz Hame'uchad Publishers: 2001 [Hebrew].

The Gate to Haskalah: An Annotated Index to *Hame'asef*, the First Hebrew Journal. Jerusalem, Israel, The Hebrew University Magnes Press: 2000 [Hebrew].

Kinds of Genres in Haskalah Literature: Types and Topics. Tel Aviv, Israel, Hakibutz Hame'uchad Publishing House: 1999 [Hebrew].

Hebrew Culture in America, 80 Years of Hebrew Culture in the United States. Tel Aviv, Israel, Reshafim Publishers: 1998 [Hebrew].

Struggle for Change, Studies in Hebrew Enlightenment Literature, Tel Aviv, Israel, University Publishing: 1988 [Hebrew].

The Age of Haskalah, Leiden, Brill: 1979.

Moses Mendelssohn: Bonds of Tradition, Tel Aviv, Aleph: 1972 [Hebrew].

Getting By In Hebrew, New York, Barron: 1984.

Two novels (1961, 1965); Eight children's books (1963–1980).